Global Trade and
Conflicting National
Interests

The Lionel Robbins Lectures

Peter Temin, *Lessons from the Great Depression*, 1989

Paul R. Krugman, *Exchange-Rate Instability*, 1989

Jeffrey Sachs, *Poland's Jump to the Market Economy*, 1993

Pedro Aspe, *Economic Transformation the Mexican Way*, 1993

Yegor Gaidar and Karl Otto Pohl, *Russian Reform/International Money*, 1995

Robert J. Barro, *Determinants of Economic Growth: A Cross-Country Empirical Study*, 1997

Alan S. Blinder, *Central Banking in Theory and Practice*, 1998

Ralph E. Gomory and William J. Baumol, *Global Trade and Conflicting National Interests*, 2000

Global Trade and Conflicting National Interests

Ralph E. Gomory and
William J. Baumol

with a contribution by
Edward N. Wolff,
New York University

The MIT Press
Cambridge, Massachusetts
London, England

This book was set in Palatino by Best-set Typesetter Ltd., Hong Kong

Printed and bound in the United States of America.

Library of Congress Cataloging-in-Publication Data

Gomory, Ralph E.
     Global trade and conflicting national interests / Ralph E. Gomory and William J. Baumol ; with a contribution by Edward N. Wolff.
       p.   cm.—(Lionel Robbins lectures)
     Includes bibliographical references and index.
     ISBN-10: 0-262-07209-2 (hc. : alk. paper)
     ISBN-13: 978-0-262-07209-0 (hc. : alk. paper)
     1. Free trade.   2. Protectionism.   3. International trade.   I. Baumol, William J.
II. Title.   III. Series.
HF1713 .G5665 2001
382′.7—dc21

                                                                                            00-056069

10   9   8   7   6   5   4   3   2

To our wives, Lilian Gomory-Wu and Hilda Baumol, and
to our families whose interest and support were vital to the writing of
this book

To Lionel Robbins

In 1994 I was invited to give the annual Robbins lectures at the London School of Economics. At that time Ralph Gomory and I were in the midst of working out the theory that is the subject of this book, so I decided that our joint work would be the subject matter of those lectures. My long association with Lionel Robbins (later Lord Robbins) and with his delightful wife Iris, Lady Robbins, added a strong personal element, so when I was invited to give the Robbins lectures I naturally leaped at the opportunity to report our work in that respected forum.

A highlight of our trip to London for the lectures was the opportunity to introduce the Gomorys, sadly, not to Lionel and Iris, but to the next Robbins generation, with whom we have been close friends for the half century since I studied and taught at the London School of Economics. At that great school Lionel Robbins was my mentor, and he and his wonderful wife became close friends of my wife Hilda and myself. I can tell many anecdotes of our meetings over the years, but that would require a separate essay. Here, I need only quote from what I have written elsewhere of the unforgettable experience of association with Lionel

Central to that experience was the man himself. Tall, massive, stately, with a sonorous voice and a leonine mane. . . . It is sheer understatement to describe him as a man with a powerful personality. His students would find themselves unconsciously mimicking his style, the personal attributes and speech patterns that recalled an earlier, less mechanized age. Yet one soon learned that his was not a domineering personality. His sense of humor was profound, and his anecdotes riveting. He was invariably considerate and kind, particularly to younger people and particularly when few others were present to observe his acts. But even more striking were his command of the language, his clarity of mind, and his incredible erudition. . . . (From the foreword to Robbins LSE lectures, in *A History of Economic Thought*, S. G. Medina and W. J. Samuels, eds., Princeton: Princeton University Press, 1998)

There were many reasons, both personal and professional, for our giving these lectures, but one is particularly pertinent and relates to Lionel Robbins. Lionel Robbins had given much thought to trade issues, and had emerged with a predisposition toward the virtues of free and unimpeded trade. We share that view. This is worth mentioning because there is some danger that this book will be misunderstood as a protectionist argument, which it emphatically *is not*. Indeed in this book we only consider free trade. Our message, rather, is that under modern free-trade conditions, there is no longer one, but rather many possible free-trade outcomes, and a country is better off with some than with others. Knowing Lionel Robbins's receptivity to new ideas and logical argument, I am confident he would not have taken umbrage at our analysis or its conclusions, and would readily have understood our true intentions. Thus the association of this book with the Robbins lectures may perhaps contribute something to clarification of its purpose.

I have had the pleasure of dedicating a book to Lionel and to his wife, both of whom we loved deeply. And, predictably, he responded in kind. Only several weeks ago I needed to consult his materials in his several books on classical political economy. On opening one of them the dedication leaped out at me: "To William and Hilda Baumol who made glorious summer of a winter of discontent" and underneath, in his hand, is written "with love from Lionel."

I am happy that this book gives me another opportunity to express my affection and admiration for Lionel Robbins.

William J. Baumol

Contents

Foreword by Richard Layard   xi
Preface   xiii

I **For the Nonspecialist: National Welfare and Trade in the
   Modern World**   1

1 The Modern Global Economy and Inherent Trade
   Rivalry: Introduction   3

2 Significance of the Multiple Outcomes That Result from
   Economies of Scale   13

3 Regions of Equilibria: Desirable and Undesirable
   Market-Based Outcomes   23

4 Multiple Outcomes That Result from Productivity
   Changes   41

5 Conclusions for Part I   57

II **For the Specialist: Further Theory and Extensions**   75

6 The Economies Model, the Equilibria, and the Number of
   Specialized Outcomes   77

7 Mapping Trade Outcomes: The Shape of the Graph,
   Beneficial and Harmful Equilibria, and the Role of
   the Market   83

8 Conflicting National Interests in Linear Trade Models   99

9 Three-Country Models and Other Complications   117

10 Predecessors   143

11 Empirical Evidence: The Persistence of Specialization in
   Industrialized Countries (by Edward N. Wolff)   163

   Notes   177
   Annotated Bibliography   187
   References   189
   Index   193

Foreword

This important book has its origins in the Lionel Robbins Memorial Lectures given at the London School of Economics in 1994. William Baumol is a leading world economist and one of Lionel Robbins' most distinguished former students; Ralph Gomory is a distinguished applied mathematician.

They have chosen as their topic one of the most important issues in the new global economy. The issue is whether, when one country improves its production capacity, this necessarily benefits all other countries—in a world of free trade. The man in the street would answer no, and the authors explain why he is right. They show why, with economies of scale or with rapid changes in productivity, a gain to one country can sometimes hurt all others, and they also explain when this will be the result and when it will not. The conclusion is that the welfare of a country depends critically on the success of its internationally traded sector.

This book is a valuable contribution to the globalization debate. It should be a serious spur to research on critical new issues of trade in today's global economy.

Richard Layard

Preface

What the Book Is About

This book is about some of the ways in which trade theory needs to be modified from the theory provided by Ricardo and his contemporaries. In Ricardo's time trade is estimated to have constituted about 1 percent of world GDP. Since then, despite exploding world output, the volume of trade *relative to GDP* has risen more than thirteenfold.[1] This surely suggests that there have been major changes in the structure of trade that require analysis, and this book is intended to contribute to the very substantial and powerful recent literature dedicated to the purpose.

It is also clear that the nature of the goods entering into international trade has changed along with the quantities. Advantages based on natural resources still exist, as they did when England specialized in wool and Portugal in wine, but more dominant today are advantages that can be *acquired*. These can be the advantages conferred by being established in an industry and gaining thereby either specialized knowledge or economies of scale or scope. There is also the possibility, in industries where knowledge is easily transferred, and where economies of scale are not significant, of dispersing production around the world to use cheap labor or other special advantages, and then to exploit the cheapness of modern transportation to deliver these goods to global markets.

Especially in this latter case one might conclude that the location of economic activity today no longer matters since international companies can repatriate their profits from whatever part of the globe houses their actual economic activities. However, in almost all cases, most of the economic benefit stays where the value is added. Profits are usually only a small portion of the value added through economic activity, and most of the value added, such as wages, remains local. It matters to a country to be the site of an economic activity, whoever may own the company.

Although the countries do not compete directly, in the way companies do, the amount of economic activity actually taking place within their borders is vital. As we will see in this book, it is vital not only for those engaged in a particular industry who may experience the ups and downs of activity directly but also for the country as a whole.

How the Book Came to Be Written

Our association now dates back four decades. It began soon after Albert Tucker, then chairman of the math department at Princeton, told WJB "There is a young man (REG) I think you should meet. He has just solved the integer programming problem." Meet we soon did, and it was not long before we were happily puzzling over the economic interpretation of the integer solution, its relation to scale economies, and a variety of other fascinating subjects. The result was an article, one that has often been cited, and after many years we still recall that collaboration with affection.

Our paths parted when one of us (REG) left academe to go on to a career in the worlds of mathematical research, science, and business (as director of research at IBM), and most recently as president of the Sloan Foundation, a research sponsoring foundation. For many years we remained aware of one another but we were not collaborators.

However in 1992 we met again, and REG explained that from his experiences in industry, he had developed some ideas on the pervasive importance of scale economies, their connection with integer programming, and their implications for international trade theory. Actually it emerged that he had already worked out much of the basic analysis and had benefited importantly from instruction in equilibrium theory from another old friend, Herbert Scarf of Yale. Yet he felt strongly that to move forward he needed a continuing partner—an economist—and of course he remembered our previous authorship struggles with great pleasure. After much discussion, during which WJB objected that he had never worked on international trade theory or directly related subjects, we finally agreed to go forward together. The result has been years of happy argument, pleasant and stimulating puzzlement, or temporary disagreement, always followed by a manuscript or more.

On Our Debts . . .

Aside from those whom we have already mentioned, there is a profusion of creditors to whom we owe deepest thanks, for direct labors on our manuscript, for helpful suggestions, or for vital encouragement. Among colleagues, those to whom we owe profound gratitude include Jagdish Bhagwati, Avinash Dixit, John Geanopolis, Gene Grossman, Peter Kenen Dan Quah, Paul Samuelson, Karl Shell, Martin Shubik, Robert Solow, and Frank Stafford. Happily the list is too long to invite us to single out the contributions of each of these benefactors. Quite aside from these personal interactions, we owe a great debt to those whose research opened up the fields that this book discusses. We are thinking especially of Paul Krugman, Gene Grossman, Elhanan Helpman, Wilfred Ethier, Frank Stafford, and G. F. Johnson. Our reference list contain the names of many others, and our chapter on predecessors, chapter 10, tries to make clear the relation of this book to what has gone before, but we will never succeed in fully describing the intellectual debt that we owe to so many.

We owe special thanks to Ed Wolff of New York University for using his unique command of data to write an important chapter of this book. Chapter 11, which he has written, offers supportive empirical evidence for the persistence of specialization in industrialized countries.

We are also grateful for the support and encouragement of the Alfred P. Sloan Foundation.

The completion of any book is a collaborative effort involving the work of many people. Prominent among these are three friends and colleagues who participated in our work with faithfulness, helpful energy, and enthusiasm. Beverly DeMaggio Newman, at the Sloan Foundation, in effect, ran the enterprise and continually prevented order from becoming chaos, though occasionally it appeared that the chaos might win. Sue Anne Batey Blackman, at Princeton, read and improved much of the manuscript, bringing to it an eye that could detect opaque sentences and paragraphs and a pen that could render them into English. Finally, Janeece Roderick Lewis, at New York University, made herself into a master of graphics and produced beautifully most of the diagrams that appear in this book. All three of these people, with whom it is so pleasant to work, helped in many other ways, but in singling out their most salient contributions, we hope we have suggested how much and how vital was the help they provided.

We must also thank our draftsman Mark Mamrega (yes, this art form does still exist) for transforming complex machine-generated graphs, calculated from particular numerical models, into readable and aesthetically acceptable versions.

The debt that we owe to our wives in sustaining this enterprise is critical: There would have been no book without them. Their contribution has been many faceted. Both Hilda Baumol and Lilian Gomory-Wu endlessly contributed ideas, reactions, criticisms, and encouragement. They were patient with our preoccupations, and through their effors they created a world around us in which the work could go forward. What more could anyone ask?

I

**For the Nonspecialist:
National Welfare and
Trade in the Modern
World**

This book has been divided into two parts for easier reading. Part I tells
the basic story—giving the ideas we are hoping to convey. We hope
that this part of the book will be read both by professional economists
and by noneconomists interested in issues such as global trade policy,
the productivity achievements of different countries, and the contrast-
ing stakes of a developed economy in its trade dealings with less developed countries and those with other industrialized economies.

We will not be disappointed, however, if part II of the book proves
to be primarily of interest to economists. Part II addresses itself to some
relevant analytic issues that have been left out of part I because they
would have cluttered the discussion and made it more difficult to
follow. In particular, part II deals with topics such as statistical evidence, pertinent earlier economic writings dealing with our subject,
and the consequences of modification of some of the assumptions used
in part I to simplify the exposition.

1

The Modern Global Economy and Inherent Trade Rivalry: Introduction

Some of the truths most dear to the hearts of economists are those that clash with the practical intuition of those not trained in the field. It does not require special training to see that foreign competition can put some domestic jobs in danger, or that once vibrant home-grown industries sometimes succumb to foreign competitors who can make the goods they once produced more cheaply or better. International trade sometimes leads to the contraction or even loss of some industries, even significant ones such as automobiles or consumer electronics, and can therefore cause hardship and unemployment. But economists generally maintain that such localized pain is more than compensated for by the availability of better automobiles or compact disc players to the large consuming public.

This conclusion rests to a considerable extent on time-honored and simple models of international trade. These models map out a world in which, through the unrestrained exchange of goods with all the gain that entails, each nation ends up producing the goods at which it is *naturally* best, compared to the other countries and products, and all the nations participating in trade benefit from the exchange of the goods thus efficiently produced. While the simplicity[1] of these models has often been attacked as a weakness, we must realize that no model of large-scale economic activity can encompass the true complexity of reality. Economics can offer valuable insights only by focusing on a few essential aspects of any situation it analyzes—those aspects that are most important for the matter that is being studied—and by disregarding the myriad other influences that are present but whose role is not vital for the subject.

However, it is also true that in the time since these basic models of international trade were first formulated, there have been major changes in the world economy. David Ricardo's world of agriculture, slow-moving technology, and tiny businesses has been replaced by a world dominated by manufactured goods, rapidly evolving technology, and huge firms. This calls for re-examination of those classical models, and such a re-examination has indeed been under way in the economic literature.[2]

In this book we will show that the classical trade models, on which so much has been built, are quite resilient and adaptable to the new conditions of the world economy. The models can be modified in ways that preserve their essential simplicity, to reflect both the effect of large-scale economic activity and the rapid diffusion of technology.

However, as modified by us, the theory shows that there are in fact *inherent conflicts in international trade*. This means that it is often true that improvement in one country's productive capabilities is attainable only at the expense of another country's general welfare. An improvement in the productive capability of a trading partner that allows it to compete effectively with a home-country industry, instead of benefiting the public as a whole, may come at the expense of that home country overall. And this harm is not the localized damage previously mentioned, loss of jobs in the immediately affected industry, but an adverse effect that is felt throughout the home country.

When we does development abroad help and when does it harm? Put somewhat loosely, our central conclusion is that a developed country such as the United States can benefit in its global trade by assisting the substantially less developed to improve their productive capability. However, the developed country's interests also require it to compete as vigorously as it can against other nations that are in anything like a comparable stage of development to avoid being hurt by their progress.

More carefully put, we will show that an industrialized country will benefit if a *very underdeveloped* trading partner acquires new industries and generally improves its productivity. It will continue to benefit until that partner reaches a level of development that enables it to play a more substantial role in the global marketplace. Usually this level of development is still very substantially lower than that of the industrialized country, but it is nevertheless a significant turning point. After this point acquisition of more industries by the newly developing partner *becomes harmful* to the more industrialized country. That country's interests are then best served by competing vigorously to maintain undiminished its still substantial advantage over the newly emerging rival. To the extent it fails to do so its economic prosperity will be diminished. Thus U.S. interests are served by progress in trading partners such as India or Indonesia, but the United States is better off staying as far ahead as possible, in terms of productivity, of trading partners like France, Germany, or Japan.

The underlying reason for these significant departures from the original model is that the modern free-trade world is so different from the original historical setting of the free-trade models. Today there is not one uniquely determined best economic outcome based on natural national advantages. Today's global economy does not single out a single best outcome, arrived at by international competition, in which each country serves the world's best interests by producing just those goods that it can naturally turn out most efficiently. Rather, there are *many possible outcomes* that depend on what countries actually choose to do, what capabilities, natural or human-made, they actually develop.

These outcomes vary in their consequences for the economic well-being of the countries involved. Some of these outcomes are good for one country, some are good for the other, some are good for both. But it often is true that the outcomes that are the very best for one country tend to be poor outcomes for its trading partner. The existence of this range of outcomes, with such different consequences for the countries involved, implies that in a modern free-trade environment a country's welfare is critically dependent on the success of its industries in international trade. The country as a whole has a vital stake in the competitive success or failure of its industries.

1.1 Multiple Economic Outcomes—Large-Scale Industry and High Start-up Costs

In the unmodified classical model the economic outcomes for trading countries tend to be unique. Free-market forces, including free international competition, will determine what goods are made where. From this unique outcome also flows a fixed and theoretically predictable degree of prosperity for each country. A country that ends up producing little of value will have little to consume at home and little to trade abroad, and will have a low standard of living.

A well-known and appropriately antique example, taught to generations of economics students by generations of economics professors, illustrates the point: If England and Portugal trade wine and cloth, Portugal, because of its natural advantages, will end up as the producer of wine, and England as the producer of textiles. Matters will never go the other way around. England's relatively sunless slopes will not produce grapes in either the abundance or quality that will enable English winemakers to out-compete the Portuguese either in price or quality. As a result English winemakers will not be able to remain in business unless the demand for wine exceeds Portugal's capacity to produce it. But England's wooly sheep, and long-established cloth-making capabilities, give it a relative advantage in textiles that does enable it to succeed in that business.

As this example illustrates, which country makes what product is generally uniquely determined in the classical economic model of trade. And that outcome always serves the economic interests of the general public in all the countries involved because a country can be the prime supplier in an industry only if it is the best supplier of that product. "Best" can mean that it is the lower-cost supplier of the item at a fixed quality level or, alternatively, that at a given cost, it is the higher-quality supplier.

It is one of the most remarkable results of economic theory that this unique outcome will tend to be best for consumer welfare and productive efficiency in every one of the countries involved.

But today's world of industry contrasts sharply with the wine-wool example that is so typical of the past. Today, in many lines of business, efficiency, *or even the ability to make a product at all*, requires firms to operate on a large scale.

There was a time when anyone with a ten-person firm could enter the automobile industry and build competitive cars. Once, all automobile companies were small and experimental, and many of today's firms are the grown-up survivors of that era. But that time is long past. Today a competitive auto company must produce on a large scale, and must operate a huge dealer and support network. Any new competitive entrant industry in another country must start on something like that scale, and that is not easy to do against those who are already entrenched.

Just as in the automobile example, much of modern technology requires activities to be carried out on a very large scale in order to be economical and competitive. Consequently entry into one of these industries, against an entrenched competitor, is slow, expensive, and very much an uphill battle if left entirely to free-market forces.

In these modern industries patterns of industrial dominance can occur simply as the result of the vagaries of historical accident. A war may force some country to invest heavily in some military product, like aircraft, or to develop a chemical industry because the country is cut off from its traditional supplier. Or a single, farseeing entrepreneur can start a company that inaugurates an industry. Such historical accidents, which can be quite divorced from any natural advantage, can give a country an edge in plants, knowledge and personnel that allows it to dominate an industry for many years.

In many of today's industries, with large-scale operations required, with difficulties of entry, and with acquired advantages rather than natural ones playing a more decisive role, the situation is basically different from the wine and wool example—*there is no single clear-cut and natural outcome*. If the United States and Japan trade in semiconductors, automobiles, and aircraft, it is easy to imagine circumstances in which the United States dominates in aircraft and semiconductors and Japan in automobiles, but it is also eminently possible for the United States to have evolved into an entrenched position in automobiles and semiconductors while Japan dominates in the production of aircraft. Or, for that matter, almost any other combination can emerge.

Any such position once arrived at, whether deliberately or by the purest accident of historical events, does not break down overnight. Market forces will preserve it because of the difficulty of entry for new competitors in such an industry. In the wine-wool world, market forces, driven by demand and natural advantages, led the world to a single outcome. In today's world, market forces do not select a single, predetermined outcome, instead they tend to preserve the established pattern, whatever that pattern may be.

As a result modern international trade analyses must deal with many possible outcomes. If many assignments of industries among countries once established are possible stable outcomes in the world economy—if Japan can be the producer of good X and Germany of good Y, but the opposite assignment is also equally viable once established—then, since there are hundreds of industries, there are an enormous number of possible combinations of production assignments that can establish themselves as the entrenched state of affairs. And all of these permutations are consistent with the free play of market forces.

Furthermore, if these disparate industry-country combinations differ in their economic consequences for each trading country—some being good for a particular country and some not so good—why should a country necessarily be satisfied with the position it currently holds? Clearly, that position is not the inevitable and optimal outcome of the working of the market mechanism. It is more a historical accident that is currently maintained by market forces. Why should a country be satisfied with the current state of affairs if it can see a way to do better?

And there are things a country can do to change its position in the global balance. A home market closed off to foreign competition is one traditional way to shelter an industry while it is growing up to a reasonable size. Such closure of the market can be natural if there is something special about the home market that the home producer exploits, or it can be the result of deliberate government action intended to foster the home industry. Either circumstance can transform the almost insurmountable entry problem into one that is merely difficult. And there is a long list of other things that can be attempted for this purpose.

While it made little sense for England to attempt to produce wine, it may make sense for a modern nation to enter the automobile industry or some other industry and establish a new and better position in the global balance that is then maintained by market forces. But this requires someone to know something about which outcomes are better. In this book we will study which of the possible outcomes are better for a given country, and we will also describe the effect on that country's trading partners.

Analyzing all these different outcomes and their effects on countries and their trading partners may seem like a daunting task. There are hundreds of industries and a large number of countries capable of entering into those industries. Do we have to consider each and every one of the conceivable matchups of industry and country? Fortunately, we are rescued from the enormous task of dealing with this truly vast array of possibilities by the fact that all these outcomes obey certain simple rules. We will describe these rules and their consequences in the succeeding chapters.

These rules will show us, however, that among the multitude of stable outcomes, *those that are best for one country tend to be disadvantageous for its trading partner.* And we mean that it is disadvantageous for its trading partner in a very wide sense. It is a sense that takes into account not only the local effects on individual industries but also the wider effects on the entire national population. It is in this sense that we find that there is inherent conflict in international trade.

So far we have discussed the different stable outcomes made possible by the difficulty of entering an industry. However, there is a second and equally important source of multiple outcomes. That second source is change in a country's ability to produce.

1.2 Multiple Economic Outcomes—Capturing the Lead through Productivity Growth

In the modern world countries can change their productive capabilities rather rapidly. We will consider the possibility of a country learning how to become good at producing something, perhaps a simple assembly process, say, shirt-making, or the manufacture of artificial Christmas trees. In contrast to our earlier discussion, we will now consider things that can be done on a small scale just as well as on a large scale and that do not necessarily have high entry costs. Nevertheless, in this case, too, we will reach the same conclusions about international trade as we reached under the assumption of high entry cost. We will again see inherent conflict in international trade.

In the world of the classical trade model, with its emphasis on natural advantage derived from climate or natural resources, it was difficult, for example, for England to become a substantial presence in wine production. However, in the modern world it is possible for many countries to learn the skills involved in making a product, and then to practice those skills until they approach the capability of the world's productivity leaders.

The skills and know-how of large, multinational corporations[3] enable them to set up shop—making athletic shoes, for example—almost anywhere in the world. The company's present employees, both management and labor, know the techniques for making athletic shoes rapidly and effectively, and they can teach new workers in other countries the assembly and other skills required to make athletic shoes rapidly and effectively in a new location. If the new workers learn to perform these skills as productively as the world leaders, and if their wages are lower than those in other countries, then the unit cost of athletic shoes will be lower in the new assembly plant than elsewhere. And its ability to compete at low cost can change the course of world trade in that industry.

The same outcome can occur by means other than the stimulus of multinational corporations. Any means of learning will do. Workers or managers can be hired from the firms that are already skilled, or people can go abroad to participate in the leading industries and learn from the leading firms. The only thing that matters is that the skills can be acquired or developed and that the resulting unit cost of production is low. If, by any of these means, the new plant becomes one of the world's low-cost producers, then market forces will keep it going, and we will have a new pattern of international trade and new national outcomes.

Thus countries today can change their circumstances and can acquire (or lose) industries through rapid alterations of their capabilities in industries that do not have high entry costs. This can lead to a new outcome in international trade. The possibility of such changes and such new outcomes is another and different source of multiple outcomes.

Remarkably enough, the resulting different outcomes obey the same simple laws as those that govern the case of high entry cost and large-scale operations. Once again, we will find inherent conflict in the countrywide interests of trading partners. Once again, the outcome that is best for one country tends not to be good for another. Once again, a multitude of possible outcomes become a possible source of conflict in international trade.

1.3   Concluding Comments

The central conclusion of this chapter is the profound contrast between the single, determinate outcome that tends to result from international trade in the classical world of small-scale industries, in which advantage is based on fixed natural capabilities, and the great and rich set of possibilities that opens up in the presence of high startup costs of entry into a large-scale industry. That same abundant set of possibilities exists even in the case of small-scale operations if it is possible for skills to be acquired, and in the modern world they can be. A grapevine cannot learn to flourish in England as well as in Portugal, but an assembler of radios can learn to assemble about equally well in many different countries.

In the classical trade model, market forces—Adam Smith's Invisible Hand—could arrive at only one outcome. In contrast, either high startup cost or learning provide the Invisible Hand with a vast array of options. This raises the possibility of attempting to modify the outcome through private acts or by public policy. History has brought us to where we are today. But people can act in the present to change the accidental outcome of history.

2 Significance of the Multiple Outcomes That Result from Economies of Scale

If the operation of free markets in the global economy always produced a unique and relatively predictable outcome for the interrelated economic affairs of nations, then there would be little that anyone could do to change it. That predestined balance of economic forces would represent our unavoidable destiny. Directed by the market's Invisible Hand, we would be fated to produce, trade, and prosper, all in a strictly choreographed international pattern. We could study, describe, and write about the details of that fate, but in the end we would either have to accept it or fundamentally reject the guidance of the free market. If, in addition, there were grounds for believing this destiny to be dependably beneficial—always serving not only the economic interests of the world as a whole but also each of the countries that compose it—then the uniqueness and inevitability of that outcome would be reassuring rather than inhibiting or threatening. This fortunate state of affairs, in which we are only deprived of the ability to tinker with something that is already for the best, is just what classical trade theory may lead us to expect.[1]

But in this chapter our review of the traditional thinking will show that these characteristic features strongly depend on one crucial assumption: the absence of widespread and substantial economies of scale (situations in which production is only possible on a large scale or is carried out most cheaply and efficiently by large-scale enterprises) or high startup costs (situations in which successful operation in an industry requires the entrant to incur a very large investment that is recoverable only after a substantial period of time). We will see that once such scale economies or startup costs become a significant feature of the goods exchanged in world trade, which is clearly true today, then instead of the single, predictable, and favorable end result, the opposite becomes possible: There are a very large number of possible production and trade relationships all of which, once established, can be maintained for significant lengths of time by market forces. Indeed, under today's conditions market forces can perpetuate whatever global balance is established in many industries rather than choosing the one uniquely beneficial outcome. And these different outcomes can have very different effects on the welfare of the trading nations.

2.1 Ancient History: The World of Preponderantly Diminishing Returns

The classical trade model used by economists reflects the world of some 200 years ago in which it was conceived. The model reflects that world especially in its assumption of what economists refer to as *diminishing returns to scale*. Diminishing returns means that as an industry increases in size, it becomes less productive rather than more.[2] Additional units of output cost more, not less, to produce.

This was in fact a very reasonable assumption when the world was dominated by agriculture,[3] for in agriculture the best or the most accessible land tends to be used first, and then, as production continues to increase and to require more land, the less productive and less accessible land is brought into use. Or, alternatively, as demand for food grows, agricultural land is sometimes used more intensively, with farmers trying to squeeze larger crop yields out of a given number of acres, something that generally entails an increase in the cost of each added unit of output. Even today we observe diminishing returns in agriculture. For example, in China farmers have used greater and greater amounts of fertilizer to raise grain. Use of fertilizer is four times what it was 15 years ago, but grain output has increased only 50 percent—a clear case of diminishing returns.

The cost of setting up a business in those bygone days was also extraordinarily low by modern standards. Historian David Landes writes, "The early machines, complicated though they were to contemporaries, were nevertheless modest, rudimentary, wooden contrivances which could be built for surprisingly small sums. A forty-spindle [spinning] jenny cost perhaps £6 in 1772; [wool] scrubbing and carding machines cost £1 for each inch of roller width . . ." (Landes 1969, pp. 64–65). The purchasing power of an English pound was much greater then, but even giving it the generous valuation of 100 times its value today, it is evident that machinery at the onset of the Industrial Revolution was surprisingly cheap, meaning that no huge investment needed to be incurred in launching a new firm.

And the firms themselves were very small. Outside of the Army, Navy, and the Church there were almost no large organizations. Most of the population was rural, and most of industry was small. As Alfred Chandler described it, "As long as the processes of production remained powered by humans, animals, wind, and water the volume of output was rarely enough to require the creation of subunits within the enterprise or to call for the services of a salaried manager to coordinate and monitor the work of those subunits" (Chandler 1977, p. 51).

It was, then, a world of diminishing returns, and in such a world, as Adam Smith, David Ricardo, and the classical economists who followed them showed in their illuminating analyses, there is normally only one possible outcome that is stable. This unique state of *equilibrium*, as economists call it, is the one arrangement of goods and services toward which free-market forces (i.e., better or cheaper producers replacing those who are less effective) always drive the economy. It is the outcome automatically selected by the Invisible Hand.

And, as the classical economists also showed, that unique equilibrium is always in some sense the best one possible. In this most advantageous situation those who can produce most cheaply in a given industry are the only ones in the industry. The less efficient producers have been driven out of that industry and are engaged in doing something else at which they can be competitive. This same unique equilibrium also does the best job of satisfying the preferences of consumers, given the current state of technical knowledge and the availability of resources. Reaching this outcome automatically is the superb achievement of the market mechanism that has rightly endeared it to economists and made them wary of interfering with its functioning.

2.2 International Trade and Diminishing Returns

Market forces yield these results because, in a world of universal diminishing returns, market forces will undo any outcome that does not assign production in a particular industry to the country that is one of the most efficient producers of that industry's goods.

Suppose that there is a country, currently not producing a particular good, that is capable of producing the good more cheaply than the current producers and therefore can make a profit by entering that industry. Profit provides the motive to enter the industry, and because of diseconomies of scale, the new producer can start off producing only a small amount of the industry's products and yet do so very efficiently—as efficiently or more efficiently than it can do it on a large scale. Diseconomies of scale mean that small is competitive. If a country is entering a new branch of agriculture, the land it devotes to it at the outset is as good or better than the land it will bring on later if its initial efforts are successful. In a diseconomies world it is not necessary to make a huge and risky leap and emerge full-grown with a large-scale industry in order to have a chance of entering the world market successfully. The new entrant can, in effect, creep in and achieve competitiveness as well (or better) on a small initial volume as on a large one.

This entry of the new competitor will drive the global economy toward a new outcome. Along the way some less efficient producers will decrease output, while the growth of the new entrant, and entry by other efficient producers will continue until the world economy settles down into a position in which only the most producing nations operate in each industry. And each of these produces efficiently enough, and has costs sufficiently low, to enable it to meet prevailing world prices.

That, in simplified form, is how the Invisible Hand of the market operates in a world of scale diseconomies (diminishing returns), always pushing the economy toward one equilibrium outcome, an outcome in which only the lowest-cost producers produce. It is an outcome therefore that always possesses a high degree of efficiency.

2.3 High Entry Cost and "Retainability" of an Industry

But whatever may have been true two centuries ago, we know that in today's world a good part of international trade consists of products that are definitely not characterized by ease of entry on a small scale. On the contrary, in many cases small-scale entry is almost impossible. Automobiles, computers, and television sets are examples. You cannot hand-make a car from scratch in your garage and compete with the large-scale production of General Motors.

And, quite aside from the necessary scale of production, it may require a long period of operation before the personnel of a new industry entrant acquire the skill and experience to make the product as efficiently as the current leading competitors. There may be new technology to be mastered, technology that is based on experience and not easily learned. Or success in the product in question may require the availability of nearby ancillary industries that themselves are difficult to establish and that the prospective entrant country may lack. A distribution network may have to be set up from scratch, knowledge of the marketplace acquired, and so on. It is not easy to compete when the competition has learned much by years of effort and experience in all these areas. And the advantage of the established industry does not need to be static. Often, considerable learning continues in an established industry. The methods and technology of production are continually evolving through large-scale learning-by-doing, as well as by continuing investment, and there is much feedback from an established customer base leading to steady improvement in product and support. This adds to the difficulties of entry by providing a moving target.

We use the term *retainable industry* to refer to any industry that is characterized by such start-up costs and the resulting difficulties for small-scale entry. A retainable industry, because of its high real start-up costs, offers the current established producers a substantial degree of protection from competitive entry, making it easier for them to retain their positions. While in industries with diminishing returns market forces favor the small-scale competitive entrant, in retainable industries those same market forces have the opposite effect. Small-scale entrants are uneconomical and tend to be eliminated by market forces while large-scale entry is hard to come by. Market forces in retainable industries tend to perpetuate the status quo.

The protection is never absolute, and no industry is perfectly retainable. The modern world has its examples in which, over time, new entrants have appeared in industries with high start-up costs. The emergence of the Japanese auto industry and its impact on the U.S. automobile market comes immediately to mind. But this is an illuminating case. The Japanese auto industry was able to start on a small scale in the protected Japanese home market. It had grown into a formidable and large-scale industry by the time its products started to appear in the United States.

This retainability attribute of modern industry is therefore important. In our analysis in this chapter, in contrast to the earlier diminishing returns or diseconomies assumption, we will assume that there is a high cost of starting up an industry that is new to a country. That is, we will discuss retainable industries and their consequences in a world of free international trade and free international competition. In chapter 4 we will extend our analysis and conclusions to industries that are characterized by rapid learning rather than by economies of scale.

2.4 When Industries Are Retainable, There Are Many Stable Outcomes

In contrast with the classical case, in an economy characterized by widespread and substantial start-up costs—that is, by retainable industries—a vast variety of possible outcomes become possible, any one of which can become and remain a stable arrangement of world production. And while some of the available equilibria score very high in terms of their economic benefits to the world public, and provide large gains from trade, others may be very poor outcomes indeed. The nature of these alternative equilibria can now be described, and we can even calculate how many of them there are.

To bring out these ideas and their differences from the classical diseconomies case most strongly, we first discuss the most extreme possibility: that all industries of the world are retainable. Then in that world, populated only by industries with high start-up costs, we will look first at outcomes in which each good is produced in only a single country. We will call such outcomes *perfectly specialized equilibria*. Of course, in real life there are many examples of retainable industries that are not specialized, where more than one country has attained the scale and expertise needed to be competitive, so that there is more than one country with a substantial market share. The analysis we are about to describe and the conclusions we will reach apply to these situations of more than one producer country as well, and we will discuss them in a later chapter. For now, for simplicity, we will emphasize the specialized equilibrium case, the case in which no good is produced in more than one country. The conclusions we reach will apply even more strongly to the case in which more than one country supplies some of the world's products, and it will also apply to the case where not all industries are retainable.

Let us first consider these specialized equilibria and see how many of these there can be, bearing in mind that any of these outcomes can be sustained by market forces. To represent the world of global trade, we will scale the world down to just two countries, the United Kingdom ("U.K.") and "France" (we choose these names only because they are familiar). Our U.K. and France are, of course, very simplified versions

Table 2.1
Number of equilibria and number of traded goods

Number of goods	2	3	4	5	6	7	8	9	10
Number of equilibria	2	6	14	30	62	126	254	510	1,022

of real countries. In contrast with the diseconomies case with its one stable outcome or equilibrium, our hypothetical, two-country world populated exclusively by retainable industries will generate many equilibria. In fact, in a world of retainable industries each and every possible specialized assignment of the task of production among different countries will be an equilibrium. It does not matter whether the United Kingdom happens to specialize in the production of semiconductors and France in the production of steel, or the reverse. Whichever of these possibilities happens to occur, the country that has specialized in one of the products will benefit from some degree of automatic protection against invasion of that field by the other country. Its large-scale production of that commodity will give its producers a cost advantage. The other country will be unable to succeed if it tries to venture into the field on a small scale because of the high costs of production, and the learning and organizing difficulties, that this entails.

Thus, in this world of retainable industries, where each product is produced by just one nation, *any* specialized assignment of products among countries will tend to persist because of the high cost of entry, and it will therefore be a stable outcome or equilibrium. And since there are an enormous number of ways in which a given set of products can be divided up among producer countries, there are an enormous number of possible different equilibria.[4] To illustrate the numbers involved (which can be determined by a straightforward arithmetic calculation; see table 2.1), if two countries trade in only 10 commodities, there will be more than 1,000 potential equilibria. And if 20 items are traded, the number of possible equilibria exceeds one million. Trade in 25 goods yields more than 33 million different stable possible outcomes. Since in the real world the number of goods traded goes into the hundreds of thousands, it should be clear that the number of potential equilibria—all stable outcomes supported by market forces—is vast indeed.

2.5   Many Equilibria: The Good, the Bad, and the Mediocre

Why should we care about the existence of this very large number of stable candidate equilibria? After all, under free trade it is still the market mechanism that eliminates high-cost producers and leads us to an outcome in which only the lowest cost producers remain. But any equilibrium with which we happen to end up is just one of many. It has a large component of history going into its selection, and very little of inevitability. Worse yet, the uniformly beneficial attributes that characterized the unique equilibrium in the classical scenario no longer obtain. Among these many equilibria there are those that are good, some that are bad and some indifferent. And they may have different effects on the welfare of the different trading countries.

The equilibrium that market forces will perpetuate is the equilibrium with which the international community will, at least for the moment, have to live. This outcome may well depend on historical accident. If Belgium happens to have gone early into the production of specialized machine tools for fax machine parts, it may have acquired a preponderant and, for the near future, unbeatable position in the field (unless there is a radical change in attendant circumstances). This can be so even in cases where other nations—if they were ever to attain the required sales volume, distribution, and reputation—could supply just as good a product at lower cost.

Influences that are fortuitous in their relation to current circumstances, ancient investment decisions, patterns of migration produced by wars or famines, or the happenstance of political orientations of yesterday's governments—all these can play an important part in determining which market equilibrium is selected by the market forces today. But though the choice may be the product of chance or history, which equilibrium ends up being selected matters today, and it matters for two quite different reasons.

First, there is the question of global efficiency. Among the many specialized equilibria that have just been discussed, each with its different assignments of products to countries, there will be many assignments that apportion these tasks haphazardly in relation to relative costs and other current economic circumstances. Japan is, for instance, a significant producer of steel and automobiles even though it has no domestic energy sources to contribute to steelmaking, and it has high wages. China, were it ever to attain volume production of high-quality automobiles, would seem to have many advantages as a producer.

It has low labor costs and lots of coal. But today, and probably for some time to come, China is not a threat to Japan's strong position in automobiles because there is so much China would have to go through to attain the strengths of volume, skill, and reputation that Japan already has.

Thus, among the many equilibria available to the market in a world of high start-up costs, there are those that are good, those that are bad, and those that are mediocre from an overall world output point of view. Yet there may conceivably be little in the market mechanism that leads it to favor the good or even to avoid the bad. Its choice among them is, so to speak, fraught with happenstance. And, once the wheel of fortune has picked one equilibrium, society only extracts itself slowly from that state of affairs. Whatever its degree of vice or virtue, the stability of the equilibrium makes it difficult to escape to a better or a worse alternative. For the move to another stable outcome can never be carried out easily. The development of a new industry is slow, involves a long time and large-scale effort, and is beset with risk.

There is a second reason why we should care about the particular equilibrium being sustained by the market, and this reason is much closer to home. Retainability means that a country with many industries can hold on to them even though the wage in this many-industry country may be very high. As we will see in more detail in the next chapter, if a country is producing more than its population's share of the world's commodities, it will have a high income and, usually, a high standard of living. If it produces a large share of the world's goods, it has much to consume and much to trade. It becomes a high-wage, high-consumption country. This beneficial effect of being the producer of a large proportion of the world's tradable industries can be very substantial, and will often far outweigh for that country the world efficiency effects mentioned in the preceding paragraph. And, equally clearly, a country that finds itself frozen out of most industries and is unable to enter will find itself with little to consume that is produced at home and little to trade to obtain goods from abroad.

So the choice of equilibrium matters both on a global scale and also very directly on a national scale. To find out which are good and which are bad, one must find a way to compare the many candidate equilibria systematically, to derive some insights into their general properties, and their relative virtues and vices. Though their sheer number may appear to make such an analysis unmanageable, we will see in the next chapter that it can be done.

We will see that these numerous possible outcomes distribute themselves into a surprisingly simple and orderly pattern that makes visible their advantages and disadvantages to the countries involved. There is nothing random about their arrangement. We will describe that pattern and show why it is universal rather than being an artifact of the particular examples we have chosen to illustrate our analysis.

Because of this simple pattern we will be able to go beyond talking about the great variety of equilibria. In the next chapter we will characterize the outcomes that offer substantial benefits to the world economy, the outcomes that provide substantial benefits to the economy of a particular country, and the outcomes that perform poorly on either count.

3   Regions of Equilibria: Desirable and Undesirable Market-Based Outcomes

In chapter 2 we saw that a world of retainable industries is character-ized by a very large number of possible outcomes, and that all of these equilibrium states can be sustained by market forces. In such a world any industry can be located anywhere. This seems to imply that any-thing is possible, that anything can happen, and that there is no order and coherence in the world economy. But this is not what we are saying. In fact, quite the opposite is true.

3.1   Order among the Equilibria

We will now show that this vast number of possible outcomes forms a significant and orderly pattern obeying a few simple rules. Certainly the number of possible outcomes is huge, but many of these outcomes are similar to each other in terms of their effects on a particular country's economic welfare, as measured in national output or jobs. For the overall national level of welfare it may not matter too much if the U.K. makes semiconductors and France produces steel (rather than France making steel and the U.K. turning out semiconductors), pro-vided that these industries are not very different in size. Many of the combinations of industries and countries will add up, in terms of jobs or contribution to national input, not to be very different from other combinations.

Nevertheless, there are some combinations that are significantly better than others for one or both of the countries. So the pattern of possible outcomes is well worth understanding.

3.2 Two Economic Implications of the Orderly Pattern of Outcomes

We will see that the pattern of outcomes has two major economic implications. The first is that there can be considerable conflict in the interests of two nations that trade with one another. This conflict does not take the familiar form of tariff wars or other protectionist battles, but it is a form of rivalry that can occur even when trade is in no way restricted and is not distorted by government intervention. This conflict centers on which of the many possible equilibria the countries end up living with in a free trade environment. This conflict occurs because, generally, among our many equilibria, those that are best for one country can be far from best for the other. This is a form of conflict that is not possible in a scale-diseconomies world with its generally unique outcome imposed by market forces but is possible in an scale-economies world where market forces tend to perpetuate the status quo.

Which equilibrium will actually occur—and which country will actually benefit and which will be relatively poor—rests on the reality of who ends up making which product, that is, on which country has which industries. The equilibrium that emerges is brought into being by the countries' pursuit of industries. The result of that conflict over industries determines which countries will benefit more and which will benefit less.

The second insight that emerges from the analysis of the pattern of equilibria is this: In a free-trade environment with economies of scale, trade is not always benign as it generally must be in the old scale-diseconomies world. When a significant number of industries are retainable, there are always equilibrium outcomes that leave some countries worse off than they would be if they were to seal themselves off from trade altogether.

It is not hard to see how this can happen. Let us imagine a country that, for some historical reason, has been slow to develop. Imagine that it exports a few agricultural crops, and imports in exchange the amount it can afford of the complex and more technologically advanced products that are supplied by retainable industries from abroad. How is this country to improve its situation? Successful entry into these retainable industries may not be possible for this country, given the difficulties we have described. If it is to make automobiles, they must compete from the start with the best automobiles from around the world, made relatively cheaply by all the leading firms helped by their large-scale production. This problem of entry is entirely different from that in a scale-diseconomies world where entry on a small scale is at least as easy as entry on a large scale.

In contrast, if this country were alone in the world, though it would have to develop its own auto industry, it might well be able to do so. It could grow that industry slowly, building on the revenue from its own national market, which belongs to it alone, because it would have no trading partners with whom to dispute the market. A similar line of reasoning applies to other industries. So a country alone in the world may be able to attain a degree of development it cannot achieve as a trading nation with well-developed trading partners. Alone, it might do better than with trade. This concept is very far from new. It is the well-known and venerable "infant industry" argument, which asserts that a country does well to nurture its newly hatched industries in an environment that is protected from outside competition. The infant industry argument applies with special force to our retainable industry model.

The point that no-trade can sometimes be better for a country than trade is worth dwelling on because it illustrates some of the strengths and some of the weaknesses of pure market regimes in which many global outcomes are possible. Let us step back for a moment and consider the matter from a different viewpoint.

Many primers in economics make the point that where trade between individuals is voluntary, except in cases where people act in error or are deceived about the facts, every such exchange must provide mutual benefits. Even a child, so the story goes, will not swap a bag of marbles for a playmate's toy truck unless she prefers the truck to the marbles, and the other child will not agree to the exchange unless he prefers the marbles to the truck. These discussions in elementary economics then sometimes jump, erroneously, to the conclusion that the same must be true of voluntary trade between nations—that two nations will not agree to exchange unless both expect to benefit. The analogy is partly, but not wholly, correct. The exchanges on the international marketplace are not determined by a nation's or any individual's conscious review of all the options but are selected by the impersonal forces of the market as affected by current industrial capabilities. And given the productive capabilities of the countries with their present abilities to produce and with no difficulties of entry, it is in fact better to trade than not to trade, as the analogy would suggest.

If the underdeveloped country were to cut itself off from trade and remain undeveloped in the industries in which it is currently not producing, it would always be worse off than with trade. What this analysis misses is that where technology is characterized by high start-up costs, there are other achievable and sustainable outcomes in which the industries that cannot get started in the presence of foreign competition can get started in its absence, and that some of these other equilibria can be better.

The possibilities we have just described—the possibility of conflict and the possibility of outcomes with trade that are worse than outcomes without trade—are important to comprehend. We need to understand the pattern of outcomes that has such strong economic implications. To make that pattern visible, we will use a graphical representation.

3.3 Graphical Representation, and Pros and Cons of Each Possible Equilibrium

In the first and simplest variation of our model, we scale the globe down to our two hypothetical countries, the U.K. and France, and to only ten industries. For each equilibrium in this small world—each possible combination of country and industry—we will calculate, by standard economic methods, the resulting national incomes. Even in this small-scale world there are more than 1,000 equilibria, each characterized by a different division of the industries between the two countries.

We focus on the U.K. and French national incomes, which consist of the amount of goods produced in each country multiplied by the price of each good (we use dollars for easy comparability). For each equilibrium outcome, once we have determined which industry is producing in each country, standard economic methods tell us the quantity of each product that will be supplied, and the price at which that good will be sold. So we can determine for each country the national income that it obtains from that outcome by first multiplying price by quantity for each good it supplies to obtain the total revenue of that industry, and then adding together all of the resulting industry revenues to obtain the country's total national income.

Each of the two national incomes so obtained is a direct measure of each country's prosperity at a particular equilibrium outcome. Added up, they also give us the total world income associated with that outcome. It is natural for our purposes to focus on the effects of trade on national income since national income is a widely accepted measure of the prosperity of a country. Using national income enables us to compare the effect on a country's prosperity of the many different outcomes.

Once we have determined the national income of each country we can, of course, easily calculate each country's share of the total world income. To do this, we use a common currency, say, dollars. For example, if the U.K. income turns out to be (equivalent to) $8 trillion, while that of France is $12 trillion,[1] the U.K. share must, of course, be exactly 40 percent of the $20 trillion total. The French percentage of the total must always be the remaining part, which in this case is 60 percent.

We can now form graphs in which a country's percentage share of world income is always plotted on the horizontal axis, and the dollar amount of national income of particular countries, or sometimes of the entire world (the combined income of the various countries), appears on the vertical axis. In this way we can literally see how the equilibria measure up against each other, in terms of their effects on our countries' economic welfare.

The first graph of the U.K./France ten-industry world is presented in figure 3.1, where we show just one of the approximately 1,000 possible outcomes in this world. Imagine that at this equilibrium the U.K. national income is $8 trillion and the French national income is $12 trillion. Then world income is $8 trillion plus $12 trillion, or $20 trillion, of which the U.K. share is 40 percent and the French share is 60 percent. This equilibrium is shown by the dot labeled A in figure 3.1. In figure 3.1 the horizontal axis simultaneously measures both countries' shares of world income: The U.K. share is measured by going from zero at the left-hand end of the horizontal axis to 100 percent at the right-hand end. The French share is what is left over after measuring the U.K. share, that is going by leftward from the 100 percent marker. It is always 100 percent minus whatever the U.K. share is.

In what follows, each of our many equilibrium points will be represented in the same way, with income share indicating the position of the equilibrium point on the horizontal axis and the height of the point representing the actual income in question. That actual income can be world income, as it is in figure 3.1, or the national income of a particular country, as it will be in some of the following graphs.

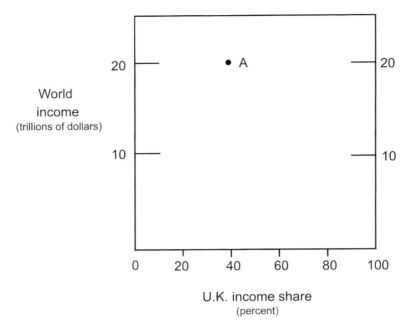

Figure 3.1
World income in trillions

We can now repeat our plotting procedure for each and every stable outcome or equilibrium that is possible in this ten-industry world of retainable industries. The result, calculated by computer, for our ten-industry model is shown in figure 3.2. This graph contains approximately 1,000 dots representing all of the model's specialized equilibria, the equilibria in which one country is the sole producer in a particular industry. Of course, there would be even more dots if we added in all the possible non-specialized outcomes, that is, if we included the possible outcomes in which some of the world's products are turned out simultaneously in both countries.

3.4   Shape of the World-Economy Graph

Just as we have promised, the 1,000 equilibria do not fall just anywhere on our graph of possibilities. Rather, the dots representing the equilibria always occur in a distinctive pattern—a clearly shaped band whose general configuration is always the same. The upper and lower bound-

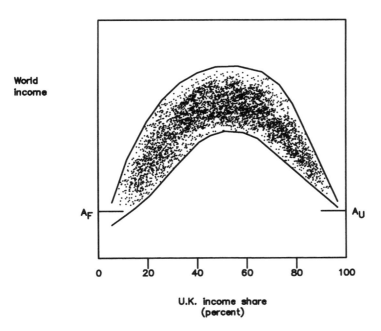

World income

A_F

A_U

0   20   40   60   80   100

U.K. income share
(percent)

Figure 3.2
Many equilibria

aries of this band of outcomes are indicated by the dark curves that we have drawn in figure 3.2.

The upper boundary line in figure 3.2 indicates the highest possible level of world income that can occur in this U.K./France ten-industry universe for each possible division (share) of world income between the two countries. The band of equilibrium points and its upper boundary are both dome-shaped, starting low at either end, where either the U.K. or France does virtually all the producing, and rising up toward the middle.

The reasons for this dome shape can be made intuitive. At the two extremes of the graph we have the equilibrium outcomes in which the world economy is organized very inefficiently. At these extremes of the graph one of the two countries is producing almost everything, that is, its share of world production and world income is nearly 100 percent, and the other country is producing little of value. It is almost as if one country were the only effective producer. An example might be an industrialized country that makes almost everything for itself and is therefore obliged to split its labor force among many industries, trading with a country that produces almost nothing that competes on the world market, except for perhaps a few very specialized crops. In such a case there is obviously good reason to expect world output to be comparatively low, and this is why the ends of the graph fall so low on our vertical scale of world income.

The much higher middle portion of the graph, on the other hand, provides to the world economy two distinct benefits that are ruled out at either the right-hand or left-hand ends of the diagram. First, toward the center of the graph, with neither country producing the bulk of the world's goods, neither country will have to fragment its labor in order to produce many items in small quantities, thereby losing the advantages that can be gained by economies of scale production.

Second, in the middle of the graph it is possible for each economy to specialize in the production of those goods that it is best suited to produce. Differences between the countries in attributes such as the availability of supporting industries, the training of labor forces, the availability of raw materials and other resources, in climate, and so on, may enable the world to produce more of everything if France produces commodities for which it is best equipped and the U.K. produces commodities for which it is best suited. But, if France produces almost every good (as it does toward the left of the graph), it may well have to devote some of its resources to production of goods at which it is efficient and some to production of goods at which it is not. Thus, in the middle of the diagram the world is better able to realize what economists call "the gains from trade"—gains that are made possible when each country specializes in turning out the goods that it can produce comparatively well. At either end of the diagram, in contrast, those gains from trade are largely lost since there we have either the U.K. alone producing virtually everything, or France doing so instead.

It is this "gains from trade" effect that causes differences in national incomes even among equilibria that yield the same, or roughly the same, share (or division) of national income between the two countries. If, for example, we look at the points representing equilibria that give roughly 40 percent to the U.K., we see that there are many of them and that they produce quite different world incomes. This is because some represent appropriate assignments of industries to countries, assignments that play to that country's strengths, while others are inappropriate assignments. Some exploit the opportunity to obtain "gains from trade," while others do not. The best assignment yields an equilibrium point that comes close to the upper boundary and the worst come close to the lower boundary, which is also shown.[2]

The overall shape of the band of equilibrium possibilities, then, can be explained in commonsense terms. However, that plausible shape has some unexpected economic consequences, as we will see next when we analyze graphs, not for the world economy as a whole, but for the individual countries.

3.5   Modeling the Individual Economies: Shapes of Graphs for the U.K. and France

Let us start with a graph, figure 3.3, for the U.K., our first trading partner. Just as before, in this graph the horizontal axis measures the U.K.'s percentage share of world income. However, the vertical axis now measures, not world income, but rather the national income of the U.K.

The graph for world income (figure 3.2) and the graph for the national income of the U.K. (figure 3.3) are very closely related. The

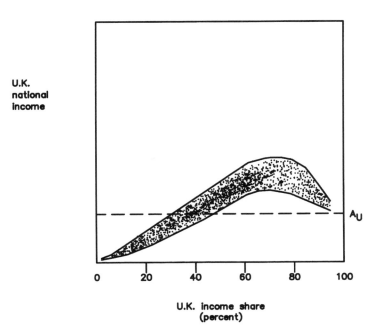

Figure 3.3
National income of the U.K.

national income of the U.K. is, by definition, equal to the world income multiplied by the U.K.'s *share* of world income. Any equilibrium dot in figure 3.2 turns into an equilibrium dot in figure 3.3 simply by plotting the former at a new vertical height, but not moving it either to the left or the right—that is, leaving it at the same share position on the horizontal axis. Figure 3.3 height is obtained by multiplying the height in figure 3.2, which is world income, by the U.K. share or percent, which is given by its position on the horizontal axis. For example, when the U.K.'s share is 40 percent and the amount of the world income is 20 trillion dollars, the height of the U.K. dot is 40 percent of the world figure, that is, 8 trillion dollars.

The dots near the left end of figure 3.3 are obtained by multiplying the height of the left end dots from figure 3.2 by a number close to zero since the U.K.'s share near that end is very small, and we see that those equilibrium dots in figure 3.3 all do have a height close to zero and represent a low national income. In the middle of the graph, where the U.K.'s share is near 50 percent, the height of each world dot from figure 3.2 must be multiplied by something near 0.5. Toward the right, where the U.K. share is nearly 100 percent, the U.K. income is obtained by multiplying world income by something near 1, so the U.K. national income points are almost as high as the corresponding world income points in figure 3.2.

The upper boundary of the points in figure 3.3 simply follows the pattern made by the points themselves. Thus the left-hand end of the U.K. boundary curve is close to zero, the middle of the U.K. upper boundary is half as high as the corresponding point on the world boundary, and toward the right-hand end of the U.K. upper boundary, where that country obtains nearly 100 percent of world income, that boundary is almost as high as the world boundary.

The result is that the dome-shaped band of points of the earlier figure 3.2 for world income turns into the hill-shaped band for the U.K. in figure 3.3. The U.K. upper boundary starts at zero at the left.[3] At first the upper boundary of the band rises steadily because the world boundary is going up and, in addition, the U.K. share of it is increasing. *Once the U.K. share passes the world peak, the U.K. upper boundary still continues to rise.* However, it rises more slowly because as the U.K. share steadily increases, total world output (of which the U.K. has an increasing share) decreases. Finally the U.K. boundary reaches a peak somewhere *to the right of the world peak* and then declines. At the right-hand end, at point A_U, where the U.K. share is 100 percent, it has the same height as the world upper bound.

The level of U.K. national income when its share of world income is 100 percent is a useful marker. Its height gives us the national income that country would have if it did not trade, since trading with a partner that contributes zero percent to the world economy is indistinguishable from not trading. This is the height that represents the national income a country can produce quite on its own. If some equilibrium point is situated at a vertical level higher than this no-trade point, A_U, then that equilibrium must be a better outcome for the U.K. than not trading. Similarly an equilibrium point lower than the no-trade level means that the country is worse off than it would be if it did not trade at all. In that case it is suffering losses rather than obtaining gains from trade.

3.6   Economic Consequences of the Shape of Individual Country Graphs

The hill shape of the U.K. graph in figure 3.3 has immediate economic consequences. For one thing, it shows us that there is an entire area filled with equilibria whose income levels are even lower than the no-trade income levels (the dots below the horizontal dashed line). Each of these many outcomes leaves a country worse off than if it had withdrawn from trade altogether and retreated into full economic isolation. These unfavorable outcomes are the equilibria near the left edge of the graph. These equilibria match the intuitive description we gave at the beginning of this chapter. The U.K., at these equilibria, supplies a very small percent of total world output or, equivalently, it has very few industries. At these equilibria it may, for example, be the marginal agricultural country trading with its developed partner that we described earlier. Its national income at all these equilibria is lower than the no-trade marker, A_U.

Clearly, the graph shows that with scale economies or high start-up costs, free trade between nations is not always and automatically beneficial. It can yield many stable equilibria in which a country is worse off than it would be if it isolated itself from trade altogether. The hill shape of the graph of the U.K.'s outcome possibilities enables us to see the connection between a country's share of world income, and its own prosperity as a nation. The location of the equilibrium points indicate that up to the point where the top of the U.K. hill is located, its national income, and hence its standard of living, will benefit if its share of world income, increases. For example, if the U.K. share is 40 percent of world income, there are equilibria with that share at which it can obtain a higher absolute income than when its share is only 30 percent. It is not only the highest equilibrium at 40 percent that is higher than the highest equilibrium at 20 percent. Most of the possible equilibria that give the U.K. a 40 percent share of world income represent national incomes above those that give the U.K. 20 percent. The entire band of equilibrium points at a 40 percent U.K. share is clearly higher than it is at a 20 percent U.K. share.

But once we get past the peak of this band of equilibrium points and continue toward the right-hand end of the graph, matters reverse. When the U.K. share of world income rises from 80 to 90 percent of the total, then the U.K., instead of becoming better off, becomes worse off. The band of equilibria turns downward, indicating that the U.K.'s standard of living, that is, its absolute income at its equilibria, decreases. This happens because near the right-hand end of the graph the U.K. has accumulated so many industries that it materially reduces the output of the world economy. In this extreme situation, where the U.K. is producing almost everything that is traded in the world, there is less world output for everyone, and even the U.K. is harmed despite having by far the largest income share. With its excessive share, the U.K. receives a large slice of what is a severely diminished world-output pie, so it is worse off than it would be if its share of the pie were smaller and the pie itself (world output) were larger. This is the penalty of an excessive share.

The U.K. graph thus shows the link between a country's share of world income and its absolute national income or national prosperity. Up to a point, share increases, which can be obtained by becoming the producer in more and more industries, contribute to the nation's prosperity. After that point, becoming the (sole) producer in more industries does it more harm than good. In other words, up to a point a country gains by increasing its share of the world's industries. However, beyond some point, further acquisition of industries harms the acquiring country.

And in every case the country as a whole is affected by the outcome. It affects not only those employed in the industries that are gained or lost. The country as a whole is affected by what the national income is, and therefore it is affected as a whole by the size of its set of industries.

A country can have too few industries, and it will then be poor; but a country can also have too many industries and, as a whole, it will be less well off than if there were somewhat fewer. In either case the country as a whole has a stake in the number and size of its industries and their success or failure.

While this describes the pattern of the equilibria for the U.K., our economic conclusions about inherent conflict between trading partners require us to know what is happening to France at each equilibrium as well as what is happening to the U.K. We can now analyze this very easily because the main features of the graph for France are almost the same as the main features of the graph for the U.K.

3.7   Shape of the Graph for the Second Trading Country

Figure 3.4 shows the set of possible equilibrium points for France. The horizontal axis is share of world income, just as before, but the vertical axis now represents the national income of France

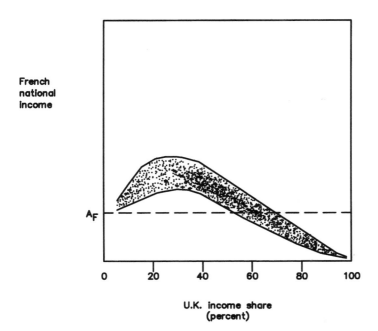

Figure 3.4
National income of France

at the various equilibria, instead of that of the world or of the U.K.

The French graph can be obtained from the world graph by the same method that gave us the U.K. graph. For the French graph we multiply the heights of the equilibria in the world graph by the French share instead of the U.K. share. The resulting graph, as can be expected, looks in most ways like the U.K. graph. It also depicts a hill-shaped band made up of all the equilibrium outcomes representing the different equilibria possible for France. The French region is again bounded by the two upper and lower curves which we have drawn in the graph to exhibit its shape.

However, the shape of the French band and its boundary curves are reversed from those for the U.K.; they are, approximately, mirror images of those for the U.K. This is so because the French share of national income is zero when the U.K. share is 100 percent, and the French share increases from right to left as the U.K. share decreases. For example, when the U.K. share of world income falls from 60 to 55 percent, that of France must rise from 40 to 45 percent. The result is that we must read the French boundary curves and equilibrium band from right to left, and those for the U.K. from left to right. The shape of the French curve is reversed from that of the U.K., and this is why they are approximately mirror images of one another.

For France, just as for the U.K. there are many equilibrium outcomes that occur below its no-trade level (point A_F). And for France, just as for the U.K., prosperity increases with an increasing French share of world income up to a point and then, past the peak of the French band of equilibria, decreases in the region of the graph where France's share is excessive.

The equilibrium point that is best for France is of course the equilibrium point at the peak of its hill, and, significantly, that point is nowhere near the share that gives the best outcome for the U.K. This observation gives us our first indication of the conflict that is built into international trade. The most prosperous equilibria for France require a large French share of world income. The most prosperous equilibria for the U.K. require a large share for the U.K. Both these conditions cannot be met at the same time.

We will be able to see that conflict even more clearly by using a graph that simultaneously shows the national incomes of both countries.

3.8 Combined Graph: U.K. and French National Incomes at the Various Equilibria

We now combine the U.K. graph (figure 3.3) and the French graph (figure 3.4), in effect by making them transparent and setting one on top of the other.

The combined graph (figure 3.5) shows the boundaries of two bands of equilibria, one for each country, resulting in a two-hill configuration. The crest of the French band is always located to the left of the U.K. crest. In this new graph the two regions of equilibria constitute two hills.[4] (We have not drawn in the equilibrium points in figure 3.5 but, in the interests of readability, have shown only the upper and lower bounds of their location. Henceforth we will draw in all the equilibrium points only when they are necessary for the discussion.)

In the graph we have drawn two vertical lines, L_1 and L_2, through the highest points of the two hills, thereby dividing the bands of equilibrium points into three regions.[5] In the left-hand region the upper boundaries of both countries slope upward to the right. In the right-hand region both upper boundaries slope downward. In the middle

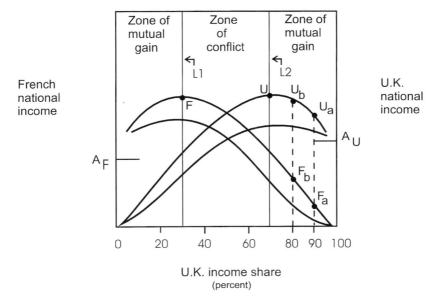

Figure 3.5
National income of both countries compared

region, the U.K. upper boundary line goes uphill as one moves toward the right, while the French upper boundary line slopes downhill.

We will turn now to the economic meaning of the three regions.

3.9   Economic Implications of the Combined Graph of National Incomes

Figure 3.5 shows that the right-hand region and the left-hand region both are filled with outcomes that can be improved upon. Both countries could gain national income by moving to equilibria that are located more toward the center of the graph. Both could move to dots that are higher up in the graph and therefore represent larger national incomes for each country. For example, in figure 3.5 we see that if the U.K. share of world income is 90 percent, that country can obtain an income as high as U_a. However, if the U.K.'s share falls to 80 percent, its maximal attainable income increases to U_b. At the same time, that decline in U.K. share also enables the French maximal income to rise— from F_a to F_b. In other words, by enabling France to increase its contribution to total production, the reduction in the U.K. share enables both countries to obtain larger total incomes. At these new equilibria the distribution of industries and income shares are more balanced between the two countries and the total world income is higher.

This is in accord with our analysis of the individual country's graphs in figures 3.3 and 3.4, where we saw that equilibria that are located at either the far right-hand or far left-hand end of the band of outcome possibilities are not good for either country. At these points one or the other nation has too large a percentage of world industries and is producing a large share of what is, as a result, a relatively small world "pie." What the combined graph shows clearly is that a move away from this situation benefits both countries.

A plausible concrete illustration of life in the outer regions of the graph is the situation in which the United States found itself soon after World War II. It was, in effect, at an extreme equilibrium point on the graph, as the overwhelmingly dominant industrial leader in the world, with its trading partners reduced in circumstances. The Marshall Plan, under which America sent massive aid to the war-ravaged countries of Europe and contributed to their recovery as trading partners, is clearly interpretable as an act of enlightened self-interest for the United States. While it led to a loss of America's share of world income, it was offset by a gain in absolute U.S. wealth as a revitalized Europe became better able to purchase exports from the United States and to offer more and better goods in exchange.

We come now to what may be the most important implication of the graphs. In contrast with the situation in the outer parts of the graph, in the central region—between the two vertical lines—the upper frontier of the U.K. region slopes uphill while the French upper frontier slopes downhill. This region contains the equilibrium points at which the interests of the two trading partners are opposed, and we call it, accordingly, the *zone of conflict*. Increasing the French share will generally increase French national income but decrease U.K. income, and increasing U.K. share will usually decrease French national income. Indeed, the intersecting and nearly mirror-image bands of equilibrium points of the two trade partners are emblematic of these countries' cross purposes in these outcomes. Roughly speaking, one country can improve its position only if the other country's position is worsened.

This large and important middle portion of the graph may well be the geometric representation of the sort of trade rivalry encountered in recent years between Japan and Germany, or between Japan and the United States, in products such as binoculars, automobiles, computer screens, and television sets, entailing the threat of acquisition of all or part of those industries by one country from another.

In the outer regions of our graph, where the two countries' upper boundaries either both slope upward or both slope downward, there are mutual gains to be had (and we call these two regions *zones of mutual gains*). Here, if the underdeveloped country acquires an industry from the highly developed one, *both* countries can gain; that is, both can raise their national incomes. If this opportunity were recognized, this outcome could perhaps be facilitated by cooperative or coordinated behavior. But in the middle region where the upper boundaries for the two countries go in opposite directions, the countries are in fact in a position of direct rivalry. Each country can achieve gains by acquiring an increased share of the world's income and its industries, but these gains must usually come at the expense of the other country.

To summarize, the trading partners face possibilities for mutual gain and possibilities for conflict. At equilibrium points in the outer regions of the graph, there are shifts in industries and changes in shares of world income that can improve the incomes of both countries. In the central region, the countries' interests are in conflict, and one country can improve its circumstances only at the expense of the other.

3.10 "Ideal Equilibria"—Are They Really Ideal?

The combined graph (figure 3.5) also shows us what may be called the ideal single nation outcome for each country—the point that is best for France, labeled F, and the best U.K. point, labeled U. These best outcomes are of course far better than the no-trade situations (points A_U and A_F at the extreme right and the extreme left of the graph). As we can see, the "ideal" points for the two nations are located, not in the middle of the graph where total world output is likely to be largest, but at or very near the top of each country's hill-shaped band. An equilibrium at the very top of the U.K. hill, point U, can be referred to as its ideal single-nation equilibrium point. At this outcome the U.K. gets its largest possible national income. However, the result for France at that equilibrium is very far from ideal. In fact, as our diagrams show, the best equilibria for the U.K. are always poor ones for France. This is illustrated by the low position of the French region in figure 3.5 anywhere in the vicinity of the U.K. peak and the similarly low U.K. income anywhere near the French peak.

If countries are to be guided by the well-known maxim, "I've been poor and I've been rich, and rich is better!"—that is to say, by pure self-interest—then one hilltop is the ideal outcome for France, the other hilltop is the ideal outcome for the U.K., and each ideal outcome for one country is far from ideal for the other. However, one can also take the position that there is something very undesirable about a world in which income is distributed extremely unequally among nations so that some countries are very poor. In the graph, as we have seen, points near the right-hand end and points near the left-hand end entail great inequality, while toward the center the income shares of the two countries are much more equal. This may well lead us to conclude that, from a world welfare point of view, equilibrium points near the center are better than points near the edges.

Countries may well choose to take this more world-oriented and less national-centered point of view. But if they do make that choice, it should be a conscious decision, not a choice made under the mistaken impression that maximizing world output automatically maximizes national prosperity. And such a country should also remember that other countries that make the opposite choice and pursue purely their own self-interest will, if they can, be choosing outcomes that are poor for their trading partners.

4   Multiple Outcomes That Result from Productivity Changes

An economic issue that persistently arouses heated debate is the effect on a nation's well-being of improvements in the productive efficiency and product quality of foreign industries. It is a subject on which business and labor often hold opposing and emotional views and on which the views of the political parties or even successive administrations often diverge. Many times it becomes far more than an abstract discussion about the effect on the nation as a whole. With jobs and the fate of particular industries at stake, the concrete instances in which an industry is threatened by increasingly productive foreign competition become the focus of lobbying and intense political pressure.

Does an increase in the industrial abilities of a trading partner drive down our wages and impoverish our workers? Do our consumers benefit when products that were once made at home become available more cheaply or in better quality from abroad? How do these conflicting consequences balance out? What is the net effect on our country's overall prosperity? These are obviously very real and very practical issues.

We will see that the analysis of our earlier discussion has prepared us to deal with these questions even in the absence of high start-up costs and retainability. These questions are once again about the relative desirability of various equilibria. The question now being asked at the national level is this: Is the equilibrium after our trading partner improves its productivity better or worse for us than the equilibrium we had before?

Our methods for dealing with the various different retainable equilibria carry over with little change to this new issue, and our economic conclusions will also be very similar. We will see once again that improvements in a very undeveloped trading partner are good for both countries, but improvements in the trading partner, once it is beyond a certain state of development, once more cause conflict in the nations' interests.

4.1 Changing Capabilities

The modern world is characterized not only by high start-up costs and scale economies, that is, by the retainability of many of its industries, but also by substantial and rapid technological and industrial change. Success in industry today is more likely to be acquired than natural. It is more likely to come from manufacturing skill, know-how, low wages, or technical knowledge, or a workable combination of these, than from any gift of nature. The ability to produce and market some good or service depends less on the presence or absence of mineral deposits and more on a superiority of learned abilities or, more accurately, on a level of learned abilities that, coupled with its wage level, makes a country a competitor in a particular industry. While superiority based on natural advantage provides stability in the industries where such advantages exist, industries whose method of operation can be learned and that do not require huge entry costs are subject to rapid changes in their competitive positions as new countries acquire the know-how and become competitors.

We have seen this in Asia. While there has been success in high-tech industries, and Japan, in particular, has entered industries such as autos and semiconductors that are high-tech and have a high cost of entry, much of the Asian success has been based on much more mundane products. Clothing and athletic shoes are not hard to make. Television sets and many other electronic consumer products are not hard to assemble. Once this know-how has been acquired, plants in many Asian countries become competitive because of their generally low labor costs. And knowledge of assembly operations, for example, can be acquired. Often, multinationals, seeking low-cost production sites, will create the plant and also train the workers.

Of course, low wages in Asia or, for that matter, in Mexico, are not new. What is new is the coupling of these low wages with adequate skills, know-how, and physical plant. The motivation for this coupling has been provided by improved market access. This means both better access to the home market via improved transportation and lowered tariff barriers, and access to the foreign market as part of an attitude abroad more favorable to foreign investment.

4.2   Changing Capabilities and Multiple Outcomes

In this chapter we will *not* assume, as we did before, that the industries considered are retainable or offer economies of scale in any form.[1] Here, instead, we deal with the case—on which the classical theory of international trade is based—the complete absence of economies of scale. Nevertheless, because we add to it the changeability of production costs through acquired technology and skills—we will reach conclusions about international trade and its effects on the trading partners that are almost indistinguishable from those that we obtained about retainable industries in chapter 3.

We will assume that production takes a very simple form, the special case often studied by economists, who call it linear production.[2] Production is said to be linear when, if it requires one labor hour to produce 6 units of some good, then two hours will produce 12 units, and three hours will produce 18. In other words, there is one fixed productivity level—6 units of output per labor hour, whatever the scale of production may be. This assumption is plausible for many industries, especially those that are labor intensive. In a simple assembly process more workers mean more production. If the capacity of the work shed is ever exceeded, another can be added at fairly low cost and the process of output expansion can continue. It is output per worker—labor productivity—that counts.

When production is linear there is no entry cost, and there is neither an advantage nor a disadvantage to doing things on a large scale. With linear production it is possible to enter new industries on a small scale and be as productive as a large-scale competitor. This is the key feature of the classical diseconomies case that leads to a single predetermined outcome in international trade, as we saw in chapter 2.

Since linear production is a particular variant of the classical diseconomies case, only one equilibrium outcome is normally possible for any fixed set of productivity levels in two trading countries. But if we consider different alternative productivity levels for the two trading countries, each different choice of productivity levels yields a different equilibrium outcome—the wider the range of different productivity levels, the greater the range of outcomes.

For example, if the United States were to have relatively high productivity levels in wheat and rice production and in making wooden furniture, while China were productive in athletic shoes and electronic assembly, we would get one equilibrium outcome. If, however, some other productivity levels were to prevail in these industries, the outcome would be different. If productivity in athletic shoes were low enough in China, the U.S. athletic shoe industry would become competitive despite the low Chinese wage, and a different assignment of industries to the countries and a different outcome would result.

Therefore, if we assume linear production, along with the possibility of changes in the productivities of the trading partners, we again have many different possible outcomes. In this way we can return to the questions discussed in the previous chapter. When there are many possible equilibrium outcomes, which are good and which are bad for the various countries? In the scenario of chapter 2 the many different outcomes were attributable to the presence of retainable industries. Here the many different outcomes result from the many different possible levels of productivity.

In chapter 3 we considered all the equilibria that are possible outcomes in a model with retainable industries. Despite the huge number of those equilibria, and therefore of different outcomes, we were able to organize the outcomes into a graph and draw some strong and simple conclusions about conflict in international trade. We will do exactly the same thing here, using linear models. We will consider all possible different productivities for the two trading countries and organize the outcomes from this vast array of possibilities using exactly the same set of graphs.

Remarkably enough, these graphs will show us, just as before, that those outcomes that are good for one country's overall national welfare tend to be bad for the welfare of the other. We will see once again that the very best outcomes for one country are always poor ones for the other. We will see once again, under these new circumstances—without retainablility, but with the possibility of different levels of productivity—that conflicting national interests can arise in international trade.

4.3   Graph for the World Economy

Because our linear production model has the key characteristic that it permits effective entry into an industry on a very small scale, with no disadvantage resulting from the smallness—it gives us for any one combination of productivity levels for the various industries, exactly one equilibrium. This one outcome will be the assignment that most efficiently satisfies the wants of consumers given that particular com-

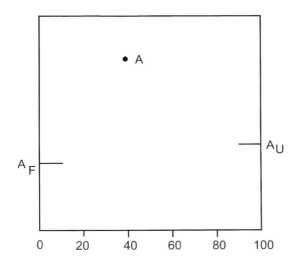

Figure 4.1
Equilibrium point, fixed productivities

bination of productivity levels. Exactly as before, we will plot this outcome as a dot such as point *A* in our graph of world income versus relative national income, with the share (relative income) of one of the countries measured on the horizontal axis and actual national income on the vertical axis (figure 4.1).

Then, if we consider a second set of productivity levels, we obtain a second equilibrium and a new dot in our familiar diagram of equilibrium points. We can go on examining different possible productivity levels and adding dots to the diagram until we have plotted all possible productivity levels.

What limits the possible productivities of these countries, and hence the possible dot locations in our diagrams? Given the state of knowledge and technology at a given time, only a certain range of productivity levels is possible. At one extreme, the floor is the limit. Of course, with sufficient inexperience, ineptitude, or lack of tools and technology, it is possible to obtain productivity levels as close to zero units of output per labor hour as one can want to consider. However, there is also a ceiling. Even with all the experience, skill, tooling and technology in the world it is not possible today to produce one million cars per labor hour.

If we are to confine ourselves to possible productivity levels, we must therefore assume, as is clearly true in reality, that at any given time there is a limit to how productive any industry in any country can be in supplying a given product. If the industry is a poor producer, it may be well below that limit. If it is doing everything well, it will be very close to that limit. There will always be a limit, and in our analysis pertinence to reality requires that we consider only productivity levels at or below that limit. Some countries do have natural advantages over others, so we will permit the limits in productivity in a given industry to be different from one country to another. Nevertheless, for each country in each industry, we will assume that there is a practical limit.[3]

The fact that there are productivity limits at a given time does have important economic consequences. If, for example, a highly developed country makes a certain good, and makes it in the most efficient possible way, it may for some time be unrivaled as a major producer. If, however, a lower wage country can learn how to achieve the same high productivity level, it can make the same good at lower cost than the highly developed high-wage country, and as a result replace the high-wage country as a major producer. If the highly developed country were not already producing at the limit of what is currently possible for it, it would be able to respond by becoming even more productive, and enhance its productivity advantage sufficiently to overcome the wage difference. But if it is already at or near the limit of what can be achieved, such an increase in productivity is not possible, and it will lose its leadership in that industry.

When, for instance, the textile mills migrated from New England to the lower-wage southern states of the United States, they used the same technology as before but now did so in a lower wage area. The southern textile mills were employing the production methods they had used up north. So there was no way for the remaining New England mills to respond with a leap in productivity and regain their cost advantage. It is this sort of scenario, portraying competition in both productivity levels and wages, that underlies the analysis of this chapter.

4.4   Shape of the World Income Graph: All Outcomes Included

In figure 4.2 we plotted the upper boundary for all the world equilibria that do not exceed the current productivity limits imposed by the current state of technical and industrial knowledge. These equilibria completely fill out the region under the curve shown in figure 4.2.[4] These equilibria represent all the different outcomes

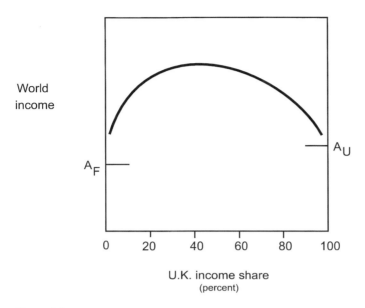

Figure 4.2
Upper boundary for the region of world equilibria

that are possible from all the productivity combinations available to the U.K. and France. Because all productivities up to certain limits are possible, the equilibria are not isolated dots, but rather fill up the entire region under the upper boundary.

Plotting these outcomes has led to exactly the same sort of dome-shaped region that appeared in our discussion of retainable industries. At the extreme right of the diagram the U.K. is the producer of almost everything that is traded in the world, and its share of world output is almost 100 percent. This can only occur when its productivity levels are almost all far greater than those of France. In fact at these equilibria France must be so relatively unproductive that even its low wage rate, which reflects its very small relative national income, does not make up for the very large number of labor hours that it takes French workers to make the various goods. Near the extreme left of the diagram the situation is reversed. A very different set of productivity levels prevails there, and France makes almost everything because its productivity levels are very high relative to those of the U.K. At the outcomes in this part of the graph the U.K. contributes very little to the world economy.

However, if both countries achieve high productivity levels, then at equilibrium both will contribute a good deal to the total output of the world economy and total world output will be much larger. Both countries will have significant shares of this larger world income, so the points representing these equilibria will be located toward the middle of the graph and will be high in the diagram, representing a large world income.

What is different in this graph, as opposed to the retainability case is that in this model it is also possible to find equilibria that are very low. Our diagram, so far, does not contain a band with upper and lower boundaries, but permits any level of low outcomes. These outcomes will occur when the productivities of almost all the actual producers are low, perhaps even extremely so. Even though in each industry a successful producer will have out-competed potential producers in that industry in the other country, its productivity still is low compared to what is possible for it. A low equilibrium point represents a generally low-productivity world, a world in which industry is generally under-developed relative to what is possible for it.

4.5   Region of Maximal Productivity

However, such a situation is not likely to persist in the modern world where industrial skills can be acquired. Countries that are actually engaged in the production of some good learn through experience how to do better, so their productivity levels are likely to rise until they approach the productivity limits imposed by the current limits of knowledge and technology.

This improvement process, driven primarily by experience, affects only the country or countries that actually are producers in a given industry. It does not apply to those that have never entered a particular industry or to those that drop out of it. The productivities of these industries, in the country that does not participate in them, are likely to remain at their original low levels. There is no opportunity to learn-by-doing in an industry that does not exist in a country.

This observation, that the actual producers in any industry are likely, in the long run, to approach their highest currently attainable productivity levels, leads us to our next topic: the outcomes that occur when the producers in each industry have attained the highest level of productivity that is currently technologically possible for them. We call such possibilities the *maximum productivity outcomes*.

There are many maximum productivity outcomes. For example, in one of these outcomes the U.K. attains its maximum productivity in the manufacture of, say, electronic pagers, while France is highly productive in other goods but has a very low productivity level in that particular good, one that is near zero and nowhere near its maximum. The U.K. in that situation will be the sole producer of electronic pagers. Another and very different maximal productivity equilibrium will arise if it is France that has the overwhelming productivity advantage in electronic pagers—reaching a productivity level near its upper limit—while the U.K. has a very low productivity level, far below its maximum, perhaps near zero. At this maximum productivity outcome France will be the cheaper producer of electronic pagers and, hence, in the long run, their only producer. All of these possible maximal productivity equilibria lie between the upper and lower boundary curves of figure 4.3 in the region we call the region of maximal productivity.

As time passes, the world economy tends to reach the outcomes in this upper region where maximal productivity is achieved in each producing industry. This is because the firms that survive and are

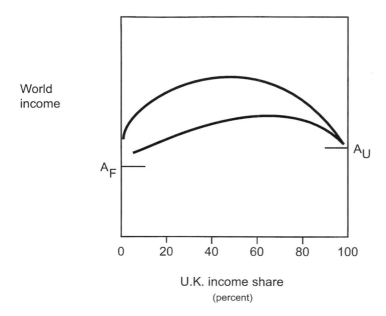

Figure 4.3
Upper and lower world boundaries of the region of maximal productivity

active in an industry tend to learn to use current best practice in that industry. Through this learning-by-doing there is a tendency for the economy to evolve toward outcomes in the region of maximal productivity. For this reason we will focus our discussion on the region of maximal productivity as we turn to the graphs for the individual countries.

4.6   Different Productive Capabilities: Graphs for the Individual Countries and the Combined Graph for the Two Countries

To obtain the graph for the U.K. from figure 4.3 which refers to the entire world, we simply repeat the reasoning we used in chapter 3. The U.K.'s income level is derived from the world income by multiplying world income by the U.K.'s percentage share of the total. If at some particular equilibrium world income is $20 trillion and the U.K.'s share is 75 percent, then the U.K.'s national income must be 20 times 0.75, or $15 trillion. Since the U.K.'s share is near zero at the extreme left and near 100 percent at the extreme right of the diagram, the U.K.'s income will be near zero at the left of the graph (because it equals world income multiplied by the U.K.'s zero share), while toward the right it will obtain nearly all of world income. The result is the hill shape of figure 4.4, with its peak off to the right of the peak of the world income dome.[5]

Repeating the same reasoning, we obtain a diagram for France (figure 4.5) with its peak off to the left of the world peak. Then, combining the two figures, just as we did before, we get the two-country diagram shown in figure 4.6.

These figures are essentially the same as those in our earlier discussions.[6]

4.7   Interpreting the Individual Country Graphs and the Combined Graph

In this chapter we have focused on the multiple equilibria that result from different productivity combinations. In the previous chapter we discussed the different equilibria that result from different assignments of retainable industries to countries. We obtain the same basic diagrams in both cases. What does the hill shape of our basic graph tell us in this situation, where we are dealing with different productivities?

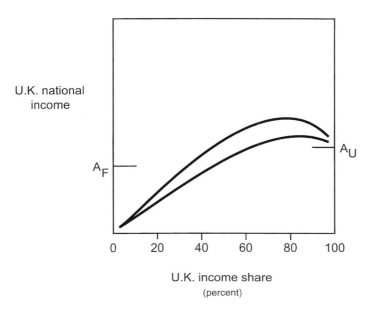

Figure 4.4
Region of maximal productivity for the U.K.

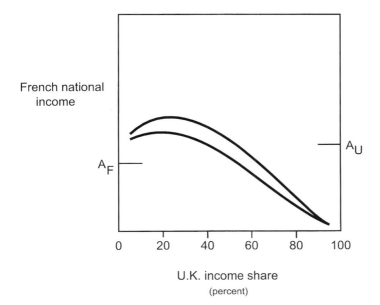

Figure 4.5
Region of maximal productivity for France

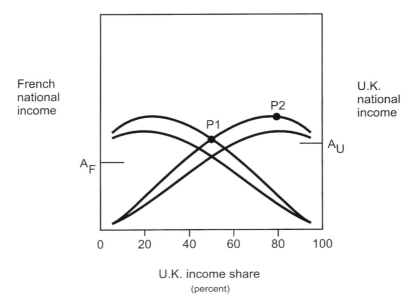

Figure 4.6
Graph for both countries with two important equilibria

The hill shape of the graphs tells us once again that up to a point a country's income, and hence its standard of living, will benefit if it succeeds in acquiring a greater share of world income. Equivalently it tells us that up to a point a country's income, and hence its standard of living, will benefit if it succeeds in changing its productivity levels so as to take industries away from its trading partner. However, once again, the graph shows us that this is a process that can go too far. If a country's *share* becomes too large, its actual national income will decline.

Similarly, if we look at the combined graph for the two countries, we see, as before, that over the range of possible outcomes that are located between the two peaks, the two countries' interests are inherently opposed. In this part of the graph an increase in one country's share brings an increase in its national income but a decrease in the national income of its trading partner. Finally, just as before, there is also a range of outcomes located between the peaks and the ends of the graph where the interests of the countries are not opposed but complementary. For example, an decrease in France's share of world income at the extreme left of the diagram increases both France's and the U.K.'s national incomes.

We see that our diagrams, applied here to the consequences of unequal productivity growth, bring us back to the main conclusions of chapter 3. Even without retainability of industries there is conflict in international trade.

4.8   Interpreting the Graphs: More Developed and Less Developed Trading Partners

What is the commonsense view that lies behind these graphs and these conclusions? In chapter 3 it was fairly clear that if history brings a country to a prosperous position in which it has a large share of world production and a high national income, it can hold that position despite its high wages. It can maintain its high wages against a low-wage competitor because it is so hard for that competitor to get started in retainable industries. In the circumstances we studied before, all the influences that lead to retainabiliy—the need for special knowledge, manufacturing techniques, knowledge of the market—provided a major advantage to an established industry. This way a country could easily outweigh its wage disadvantage and hold on to an industry. But what is the corresponding explanation here? In the model of this chapter there is no retainability, so new producers can enter an industry on a small scale without being placed at a disadvantaged by that small size. How then can there be outcomes that give a prosperous high-wage country a large share? How can the high-wage country hold on to its industries at such an equilibrium when it can be challenged by low-wage aspirants?

The answer is that this can be achieved by that wealthy nation only if its trading partner is not a fully developed industrial nation. In other words the trading partner cannot have attained its maximal productivity in all industries. If the U.K. is fully developed in most of its industries, while France is not, so that France is not the industrialized partner that the name "France" suggests but is in our hypothetical illustration rather undeveloped, then the U.K. can pay a high wage and still be the dominant producer in most industries. Its high wage coupled with high productivity enables it to out-compete France in most industries because France has not attained its best possible performance in those industries. In those industries France is characterized by low productivity as well as low wages.[7] This mythical "France" resembles many

Asian nations that have attained high levels of productivity in only a few parts of their economies, while combining low wages with low productivity in many other sectors.

In figure 4.6, which deals with two countries whose labor forces and maximum productivities are different but not very different, we draw attention to two outcome points of particular interest. One of them, marked P1 in the figure, is the equilibrium obtained when both countries are fully developed. P1 shows the U.K.'s national income at that equilibrium. The other, marked P2, is the outcome for the U.K. reached when it alone is fully developed and its trading partner's productivity levels permit the U.K. to attain its highest national income. In other words, we can say at this point that France is the U.K.'s ideal trading partner.

A detailed analysis of P2 shows exactly what we should expect from the previous discussion and indicates what makes this particular outcome good for the U.K. The U.K. has a large share of the world pie and large actual national income at equilibrium P2 because at P2 France is not fully developed. It has reached its maximal productivity in only a few industries. Because of its low wage, France captures only those few industries in which it is fully developed. But in the remaining large number of industries France is undeveloped. In these industries it has low productivity, and the U.K., despite its large share, high national income, and high wage, has productive superiority sufficient to make it the cheaper producer, and therefore the actual producer in these industries. In this way it captures a large share of world income. P2 clearly is a very good outcome for the U.K. and a very poor outcome for France.

An example of such an equilibrium state is a country that has a number of developed (though not necessarily high-tech or retainable) industries trading with another country that is mainly agricultural and has only a few export crops. While such situations have existed for long stretches of time in the past, they also can change, and we have seen many such transformations in the past two decades, especially in parts of the "tiger" economies of Asia.

As figure 4.6 shows, if the less developed country (France, in the graph) increases its productivity and starts to move toward fuller development from its state at P2, it ceases being the ideal trading partner. Such development is good for France but bad for its fully developed trading partner. That is, the resulting move to the left in the graph moves France to a higher point on its income curve and moves the U.K. to a lower point. Thus the common view of many noneconomists, and some leading economists as well, that improvements in productivity in a foreign industry can be damaging to one's own country is, under these circumstances, exactly what our analysis confirms.

4.9 Rapidly Evolving Industries

Our discussion so far makes it seem that there is nothing a country can do to retain an advantageous position. If at some time its trading partner is relatively underdeveloped, it provides an equilibrium near the peak of the home country's hill. But if the trading partner gradually becomes more developed, there appears to be nothing that the home country can do but watch sadly as the trading partner prospers and its own national income declines.

However, this is not always so. In our analysis we assumed that the limits on productivity were fixed, and this is a reasonable assumption for many industries in which there are only small annual increases in productivity that are not large enough to protect against a low wage entrant whose productivity levels grow to somewhere near their maxima. There are nevertheless industries in which the pace of evolution is so rapid that it is difficult for new entrants to reach the rapidly improving maximum productivity levels. The evolution of the biotech industry and of the Internet companies are examples of this sort of rapid change, which can be copied, but in which it is difficult for others to keep up with the rapid pace of improvement.

A country leading in an industry in an area of rapid change can continue to press its advantage and keep ahead even though its trading partner is also learning. If the leading country continues to keep its relative advantage, it can remain the producer even though its trading partner is getting better too.[8] This view provides some basis for the often instinct-based preference for high technology industries. Perhaps a better description of what is needed is rapidly evolving industries, industries in which productivity is rapidly improving.

It is also possible, if history is a guide, for industries going through a period of rapid change and rapid evolution then to enter into a phase of consolidation. They turn from easy entry and rapid change into a collection of much larger survivor companies whose names are known and trusted and whose scale, in a more settled industry, may well give them an advantage. There may well be a long-term payoff to a country trying to lead in rapidly evolving industries. They will be there when things settle down and those industries become more retainable.

4.10   Concluding Comment

The graphs for different productivity-generated outcomes look the same as those in the previous chapter, where retainability was the issue. Our graphs driven by productivity change have the same basic shapes as the corresponding graphs in chapter 3. They have the same economic implications about the possible conflict of national interests in international trade. We encountered conflict and cross-purposes in the case of retainable industries—industries with substantial scale economies or start-up costs. Now, these same conflicts are also seen to emerge from a model that focuses upon a second crucial attribute of modern industry: rising productivity attributable to technological change, imitation, and the acquisition of skills.

Our graphs show us that the basic message of this chapter is the one that we outlined at the start of chapter 1 and have seen confirmed in chapter 3 where we considered economies of scale and retainable industries. An industrialized country will benefit if an *underdeveloped* trading partner acquires new industries and generally improves its productivity. It will continue to benefit until that partner reaches a level of development that enables it to play a more substantial role in the global marketplace. After this point acquisition of more industries by the newly developing partner *becomes harmful* to the more industrialized country.

Our discussion also suggests that there may be actions that a country can take, even in this case, to improve its situation. The model suggests, for a developed country, a focus on rapidly evolving industries and, for a less developed country, a focus on industries where productivity advances are *not* occurring rapidly.

5   Conclusions for Part I

Our goal in this book has been to show how some important aspects of modern industry have changed the way international trade allots world output among nations. These new aspects—the large scale of industries and the acquisition of industrial skills—have presented trading countries with a wide range of different possible outcomes. Countries no longer are driven by market forces to accept a unique and predetermined position in the global economy, one that is virtually dictated by natural endowments. However, this opportunity to choose among different outcomes and to work toward those that are preferred has also introduced new types of conflict in the national interests of trading partners.

This revised picture of the world, with its new possibilities, raises many questions. It invites consideration of what a country's goal ought to be, and when that question is answered, it leads us to inquire about the means by which a country can act to reach that goal. It also raises questions about the role of government and of companies in contributing to national welfare. In this chapter we discuss these issues and in some cases we offer answers. However, those answers are intended more as illustration than as prescription. It is our hope that others, thinking along these lines, will find better methods and better policies so that our re-examination of international trade can be translated into actions that benefit a country.

The very first basic question raised by our model of international trade goes far beyond the bounds of economics. Should a country act exclusively in its own self-interest when that objective, successfully pursued, inflicts a low standard of living on its trading partner? Economic reasoning cannot shed much light on the appropriate answer, and we have not even attempted to explore that choice here. Our position is only that a country's choice should be conscious and informed, not one made under the illusion that trade is either uniformly benign or inherently evil. The choice should be made with awareness of the trade-offs actually involved.

But there are many other pertinent questions that are more amenable to analysis. We have seen that whether a country gains or loses from the development of its trading partner depends on its share of world output. If the U.K. has too large a share of national income, it gains from its partner's development. If it has less than its hilltop share of national income, it is more likely to lose from its partner's further development. Clearly, an important question follows: How can a country know where it is currently positioned in our diagram, the diagram of national income versus income share, that has played such an important role in our analysis? Depending on where it is in the diagram, a country might well conclude that it needs more industries or, alternatively, that it would be better off with fewer industries. How is it to know where its present outcome is located in the diagram?

If one succeeds in answering that question, so that a country knows both where it is in the range of possible outcomes and where it wants to be, then we face another issue: Should governments be involved in trying to move a nation toward another and better outcome, if indeed a better outcome can be decided upon? In a free-enterprise economy trade is, after all, the province of firms and industries, and the results of trade depend on the individually determined actions of many individual firms.

The argument for government interest in patterns of international trade should be distinguished from advocacy of active government participation. The basis for government interest stems from the fact, amply demonstrated in our diagrams, that the patterns of industrial production resulting from international trade affect the standard of living of everyone in the countries involved. The success or failure of an industry shifts the equilibrium outcome. The result is not of parochial interest only to the companies or the industry directly involved, but, also, to the country as a whole because of its effect on national income. The issue of a direct governmental role in industry is much more complicated: As we all know, government actions can be harmful as well as helpful.

Finally, if a country knows both where it is and where it wants to be in our diagram and realizes that it is a national and not only a parochial problem, one must ask how it can move to a better outcome. Should it create or destroy, benefit or handicap, some industries in order to move to that improved outcome? Or, are more attractive courses of action available? These are the questions that we address in this final chapter of part I of this book.

5.1   How Does A Country Know Where It Is?

We have modified the classical model by introducing industries that require large-scale operation, or alternatively, by incorporating the effect of changes in the productivity capabilities of the industries of the trading countries. In both cases we found that the points representing the various possible equilibrium outcomes in our basic graph distribute themselves into hill-shaped zones. Whether the hill shape is attributable to large-scale operations or acquired skills, the best a country can hope to achieve, if it exclusively pursues its own interests, is to end up at the peak of its hill. These are the equilibria represented by the two dark dots in figure 5.1.

If a country's share is larger than its income-maximizing level, then it is in what we referred to earlier as the zone of mutual gain. A country in this zone will then tend to benefit if it loses some income share, and

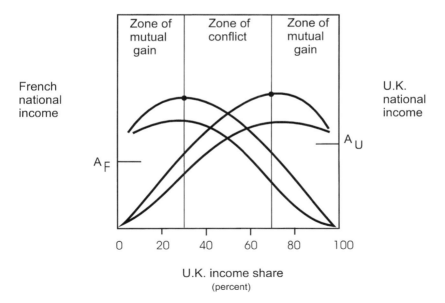

Figure 5.1
Zone of conflict and zones of mutual gain

hence some industries, to its trading partner. This is the case where it is, indeed, legitimate to claim, in the familiar phrase, that freer trade will make the other country "a better market for our goods." In fact, in this case, both countries stand to benefit from the change.

However, if a country's share of total world income is smaller than the one that corresponds to its hilltop position, then it is either in the zone between the two peaks, which we referred to earlier as the zone of conflict, or it is to the left of that zone, in the second part of the zone of mutual gain (figure 5.1). In the zone of conflict the position of the two countries is inherently a competitive one. Each country can probably benefit if it succeeds in increasing its share of the world outputs of various industries and becoming a producer in a larger number of industries, thus emerging as a higher-wage country. However, while this is likely to benefit the country that succeeds in this process, its gain will usually come at the expense of its trading partner.

This discussion immediately leads us to ask how a country can determine in which regime it actually finds itself. How can it determine whether gaining or losing industries, and hence share, really promotes its own interests? Only by knowing the position of the current equilibrium in the diagram can it ascertain the effect of changes in industries on its own welfare and that of its trading partner. Which of these diametrically opposite changes, gain or loss of industries, is desirable in its situation?

Determination of the country's current position in our fundamental diagram must be faced up to, whether that country is purely pursuing its own national interest or takes a more global view. While no simple and definitive method of determining that position is available, there are some reliable indicators.

5.2 A Guide to Location on the Map of Outcomes in Reality: Wage Differentials

In chapter 4 we saw that the share of world income that is constituted by the national income of a country is closely connected to its wage rate relative to that of its trading partner. The greater the share of world income that a country can garner (by virtue of its possession of a great many retainable industries, or its superior productivity in nonretainable industries), the higher the wages that it can pass on to its workers. We can see in figure 5.1 that, at the equilibrium point located at the apex of the U.K.'s income hill, the U.K. has captured a large share of industries (approximately 70 percent of the total) relative to France. At this peak point the U.K. obtains its highest possible national income and can pay very high wages to its workers. France's situation at U.K.'s peak outcome is miserable indeed: it ends up with a small share of industries and a small portion of world income. Its income at that point is meager in comparison with the income of the U.K., its out put is low, and it is forced to pay its workers poorly. By our calculation (for countries of roughly similar size), the U.K. hilltop in our diagram is usually located so that the U.K. pays its workers two to four times as much as its trading partner pays its workers. So, in wage-rate terms, a country's ideal trading partner (its partner at its own best outcome) is characterized by wages ranging from 50 to 75 percent below its own wages. This observation about comparative wages in the diagram offers some guidance to a country striving for its own ideal position, helping it to assess its current trade situation.

The wage-rate yardstick (or some approximation to it) can help us to determine how trade partners measure up in the real world, telling us, for example, which countries lie in the zone of conflict and which in the zone of mutual gain. However, since the different wage rates for each country are not easily comparable, we will use, instead, data for income per person (or per-capita) as a reasonable approximation.[1] These data indicate that per-capita incomes for many European countries are well above 75 percent of U.S. per-capita income. For example, Switzerland's real per-capita gross domestic product (GDP) is 92 percent of U.S. real per-capita GDP, Norway's is 85 percent, Germany's is 84 percent, Denmark's is 79 percent, France's is 79 percent, Belgium's is 76 percent, the Netherlands' is 75 percent, Austria's is 73 percent, the U.K.'s is 73 percent, and Italy's is 72 percent.[2] This means, as we have just seen, that these countries may be considered to be in the zone of conflict with the United States.

Similarly, developing and partly developed countries tend to be found in the zone of mutual gain. For example, there is the Asian group including Thailand, Indonesia, Pakistan, China, and India, and the Latin American group including, among others, Colombia, Ecuador, Peru, and Bolivia. Among the members of the African group are Congo, Morocco, Nigeria, Ghana, and Uganda. Their per-capita GDPs lie in the range 3 to 22 percent of U.S. per-capita GDP. Of the 101 countries for which the data are available, 68 fall in this low-income group, thus providing plenty of opportunity for acts of enlightened self-interest by the world's wealthy economies.

There is also a small, in-between, group that has a per-capita income range close to that of an ideal trading partner for the United States. This group includes South Korea, Greece, Venezuela, and Mexico. These countries are certainly not highly impoverished, but they are still considerably behind the most prosperous.

What these data suggest intuitively for the United States is that it will gain if economies in South America, for example, increase their productivity, even in industries where that improvement causes them to take business away from U.S. industries. Such developments are beneficial both to the United States and to South America. On the other hand, these data indicate that such a move by western Europe or Japan will be harmful to our economy. In fact, if we can acquire industries from these industrialized areas, we will increase our income but we will do so at their expense.[3]

5.3   Moving to a Better Equilibrium

Having discussed the location of the global equilibrium, let us proceed to the next problem: How can a nation improve its share of world income, that is, how can it move toward its most advantageous share of industries? For a country that is underindustrialized relative to its principal trading partners, a gain in share in any industry is a good thing. If its relative position varies from one trading partner to another, the country may find it desirable to change its position selectively, seeking to gain industries from more affluent nations, and encouraging the development of trading partners that are less prosperous to enter into more industries.

It is important here to emphasize again that the effects of all these variations of industrial share matter a great deal to the nation as a whole. Growth in the output share of a particular industry can benefit the entire country—the expanding industry itself does not capture all the desirable consequences of that growth. But since industries or individual companies cannot expect to reap all of the beneficial effects of these changes in industry share, they probably will not devote to that goal the full amount of effort and resources that would maximize the benefits to the country as a whole. This familiar line of reasoning favors some form of supplementary incentive beyond that offered by market forces alone. While this is clear in principle, the problem in reality is to find something that actually works, something that actually succeeds in expanding or acquiring retainable industries.

Government aid designed to encourage such growth of an industry, whether nascent or not, is a path many less developed countries have followed, without the benefit of this analysis and often over the protests of the international economic community. For some countries this strategy has worked, and for some it has not. France, for example, had a long-term program supporting a French computer industry, and the same industry was chosen for government assistance by Brazil and by Japan. Of these three expensive programs, only the Japanese attempt was successful. The aeronautical airframe industry has been targeted by the European Airbus consortium, and a semiconductor industry has been developed successfully, first in Japan and then in Korea. Most of these government-supported efforts have involved high-tech industries that we can regard as retainable industries because their initial costs were enormous and their scale of operation is very large. Even today, few countries have been able to mount successful entry into these industries. Most countries have not even considered attempting to do so.

Considerably more common has been growth through acquisition of the skills that enable a country to exploit its low wages and enter industries that are not retainable. A good deal of Asian growth has involved electronics assembly, mechanical assembly (low-cost printers), production of athletic shoes, manufacture of clothing, artificial Christmas trees, and the like. Much of the learning involved has been indigenous, and much has also derived from multinational firms that set up plants to make use of the low labor costs in these countries. This type of growth has the advantage that it requires from government only a permissive environment rather than a massive directed effort.

5.4   Potato Chips versus Computer Chips:
Which Industries Are Promising Targets?

From what we have said so far it would appear that all industries of the same size are equally desirable as prospective acquisitions. Their contribution to output share is, by definition, proportionate to their size, and whether lost or gained, it is industry share that matters. Some countries have focused their attempts to increase their industry share on high-tech, retainable industries, but as we remarked above, this is a difficult road. Are these retainable industries better than nonretainable industries, however? Or is it really true, to paraphrase a former U.S. government official, that the potato chip industry is just as good a target as the computer chip industry? Do they not promise equal benefits, according to our analysis?[4]

While gains in share in each of these industries may, at least in the short run, contribute comparably to national income, expansion in potato chips or, more realistically, in athletic shoes, may well prove harder to retain. In computer chips there is far more special knowledge to be gained from experience—through learning-by-doing. A far larger initial investment both in learning and in equipment is required, and technology continues to advance at a far faster pace, thereby offering the incumbent industry the opportunity to keep moving ahead of a prospective entrant. But if an entrant can get into the field, advance to the technological and production frontier, and establish a reputation for making these intricate and sensitive products reliably, it becomes difficult to beat. In short, because the manufacture of computer chips is a retainable industry, resources spent on its establishment are apt to offer more enduring benefits to the economy.

This contrasts sharply with resources spent to facilitate the acquisition of a substantial position in athletic shoe production by domestic manufacturers. The technology and production methods are relatively static. For a developing country, the advantage may last for a worthwhile period, that is, until the prevailing wage in that country rises enough to allow it to be undercut by some other nation whose wages are now lower than its own. For a developed country, money spent on government subsidies to an industry such as athletic shoes does not promise a lasting change in productivity or establish a retainable position. Competitiveness may not outlast the subsidy. From the nation's point of view the benefits, if any, are likely to be short-lived.

This is an example of a more general point. While it is share of world income that matters primarily in our model (regardless of the identity of the industry that contributes it), industries in which a retainable position can be established are those that offer the most substantial prospect of a long-term gain in share. Thus, the analysis of this book suggests, for those countries that are capable of it, a focus on retainable industries—those in which share gain can have a more lasting effect. This may, for example, lead to emphasis on high-tech industries. In a similar vein it suggests a focus on industries of the type described in chapter 4, industries whose productivity limits are expanding rapidly and which may mature into retainable industries.

5.5   Choosing High-Benefit Industries: Bureaucratic Capabilities, History of Industrial Guidance, Political Roadblocks, and Innovation

While the governments of some nations have successfully organized, cajoled, and even forced their home enterprises into entering existent retainable industries, most such efforts have not succeeded. Those that have achieved their goals are countries with a strong tradition of powerful government and an unambiguous history of industrial policy, plus a skilled and prestigious bureaucracy, able to carry out that policy. This is a set of circumstances that seems far from the conditions that prevail in the United States. Indeed, the U.S. tradition runs in the opposite direction: It has had no conscious industrial policy, and its government bureaucracy has, with some exceptions, never aspired to a close, cooperative relationship with industry outside of the arena of national defense. Even if it were desirable, a path of very active government guidance of and collaboration with industry is probably unworkable for the United States.

In addition there still remains (in all countries, but perhaps most markedly in the United States) what may be called the "political problem." Even economists who agree that there is in principle an appropriate role for the government in encouraging, guiding, and financing industrial development have recoiled at involvement of the U.S. government, in light of its traditional patterns of behavior. They have argued, on the basis of considerable discouraging experience, that whatever dispassionate economic analysis may indicate about the identity of the industries that are appropriate candidates for encouragement and assistance, the government's selection will in actuality be influenced heavily by political pressures. Those pressures have tended to drive government to favor "sunset" industries—where employment and investments are most threatened by market developments or foreign competition, and whose prospects for the future are the least promising—because it is there that the greatest pain is likely to be felt, and the cries for public support are consequently sure to be loudest.

Although the United States may, perhaps, lack both the dedicated bureaucracy and the political will to rely on effective government backing for entry into an existent retainable industry against entrenched competition, there are other ways that it can pursue such industries, ways that exploit the country's strengths and avoid its weaknesses. One of the historic strengths of the United States has been the large scale and the isolation of the U.S. economy through much of its history. Our domestic steel industry did not face a powerful threat of imports as it was maturing. Exports of steel to the United States were not a viable option for the European economies that were so far away.

The United States also has a history of practical innovation. Its early role in electric power and telephones, automobile mass production, and radio enabled the United States to be in on the beginning of these endeavors and to grow with them as they matured from small early stages into giant retainable industries. That tradition continues today in biotechnology, computers, software, and the Internet.

Although the U.S. has avoided any explicit industrial policy, it has nevertheless benefited in recent times from its consistent support of basic research, an ongoing commitment of government resources that has helped the United States launch an extraordinary number of major modern industries and emerge with a commanding position in them. Recent examples are the biotechnology industry and, very recently, the vast array of electronic communications of the Internet. The U.S. may not have skilled and experienced government personnel who can help to shape up an industry against an entrenched competitor, but it does have a long precedent of spending to encourage basic research. This has helped the country to be in on the start of new industries.

This research base, coupled with another U.S. strength—the venture capital system (the private network of investment firms and individuals that stands ready to finance risky, but highly promising, new undertakings)—has made it possible in the very early stages of high-tech industries to spawn small, entrepreneurial companies, most of which die, but some of which grow and form the nucleus of a new industry. For the United States it has been far easier to gain retainable industries by "growing" them from scratch, rather than by entering late into a retainable industry that is already developed elsewhere.[5]

Clearly, then, government support of basic research, coupled with its venture capital system and a culture that emphasizes entrepreneurship, seems a promising way for the U.S. to preserve and promote its economic position through retainable industries. Of course, from this point of view basic research is not an end in itself. Rather, it serves as a way of entering early into retainable industries. This implies that further development of the fruits of basic research, transforming them into products for the market, can also make a vital contribution. But just what is to be done here is a subject for debate. Some feel that government's role should stop at support of basic research, believing that the free market can best be left to itself to take care of things after that. Others want government to help in the translation of new research findings or nascent technology into working products. Here, we want only to draw attention to the *goal*, not the means to it. The goal is to exploit the U.S. strength in basic research, turning its results into the creation of successful industries that contribute to the nation's standard of living.

There are many industries for which free-market forces have already produced these results or are currently doing so. While government support helped start the Internet, once it was going, government controls, notably the exclusion of commercial entities from access to the Internet for many years, probably slowed widespread adoption. The free market, largely through venture funding followed by public stock offerings, has now taken up this activity with great enthusiasm.

But in other industries the story can be very different. For example, recent progress in the fundamental understanding of metallurgy and composites has not rapidly found its way into the powdered metallurgy industry, a collection of very small companies with no research of their own and little or no contact with universities. It seems appropriate to seek ways to help that sort of translation, not for industries where it is already happening on its own, but for those where it is not. An industry-by-industry approach seems appropriate here, with the means of translation from basic research to viable commercial use varying from industry to industry.

However, it should also be clear that, as helpful as it is to be in at the birth of an industry and to grow up with it, a country may also be driven to defend its position when such an industry does become a large and important contributor to national income. Semiconductors, steel, and automobiles are all examples of industries in which the United States had a major role from their earliest days. Those positions, at later dates, were subjected to major challenges. In these three cases the U.S. government actually did intervene, often over the protests of some advocates of the free market. In the case of semiconductors, the federal government funded half of Sematech, an industry consortium. In the other two cases, the government encouraged "voluntary constraint" on the part of countries sending steel and automobiles into the United States.[6] In each case these U.S. industries gained time, went through some difficult readjustments, and emerged as somewhat smaller but still substantial industries and major contributors to the national income.

Again, we emphasize that the theory described in this book indicates that such government intervention, if successful and if justified by the position of the country in world trade, need not serve only the interests of the industry in question. Our model of international trade suggests that preservation of a retainable industry, if the country has a share of national income less than its peak share relative to its trading partners, is in the national interest. It has been helpful, from the U.S. point of view, that retention of an established position, as in the cases of semiconductors, steel, and automobiles, proved to be a task far less difficult than the creation of an equivalent industry from scratch.

5.6   Increasing the Share of World Income: Nonretainable Industries

So far we have discussed the acquisition of retainable industries as a means to increase a nation's share of world income. These industries are often composed of those large, prestigious enterprises that the industrialized countries of the world are at pains to obtain. But we should also consider industries that are not retainable, the unglamorous industries in which scale of operation is not necessarily large. In chapter 4 we saw that increases in productivity abroad, coupled with lower wages, can put an end to the competitiveness of a home industry. If the home industry is already operating at maximal productivity, there is no cure for this loss within the regime of free trade that we have discussed in this book. Although support in the form of subsidies is often attempted in response to political pressure, this does not increase overall national income but merely transfers income from one group of people to another. Such an industry will eventually still be lost when the subsidy stops. In these cases the nation can try to minimize or avoid these losses by seeking to ensure that the home country's productivity in each such industry is in fact up to world standards. If nonretainable industries are producing at less than their maximal possible productivities, such improvements can postpone the loss of such industries and in some cases their loss can be avoided altogether.

The means for bringing productivity up to snuff vary. Industries that consist of small companies can be helped by an industry association that gathers information on the most productive methods from around the world. In some cases government or the industry itself can support re-education and training of the workers in the industry. Again, an approach suited to the needs and attributes of the individual industries probably is best, and some industries will prove to be beyond help. But the goal is clear. Industries should, where possible, be encouraged and possibly helped to approximate maximal productivity. If government can find effective ways to help this happen, that is in the national interest, not only in the parochial interest of the industry involved.

There is, of course, the other side: the instances when the home country finds itself in the zone of mutual gain, not the zone of conflict, with one of its trading partners. Then it serves the home country's own interest to help its trading partner's development. Today multinational corporations do this automatically and without thought of the consequences for any particular country, including their home country, when they build plants abroad. Training and education of workers and students is another variety of such aid.

5.7   More General Government Actions to Support Industry

In addition to industry-specific approaches, there are government actions that improve general conditions and thereby can help many industries to succeed. Such measures leave the free market to determine which industries make most effective use of the resulting opportunities. Government outlays on infrastructure—such as roads, or an advanced educational system—are not aimed at particular industries but benefit many. Of course, such expenditures benefit some industries more than others. Those that build roads and those that construct or maintain the plant and equipment of universities will gain directly from such government support. And an advanced educational system will more likely benefit the computer industry more than it does coal mining. Infrastructure development thus represents yet another compromise between market choice and public-sector choice of the industries to be encouraged.

5.8   Implications of Our Analysis for
Less Developed Trading Nations

Some of the most prosperous countries in the Far East have followed a pattern of rapid growth in productivity focused upon only a small number of industries rather than a fairly uniform increase in the overall productivity of the economy spread thinly over a large number of industries. This focused pattern is consistent with what our analysis suggests as the most promising approach available to a developing country that is determined to achieve a lasting gain in its income level by acquiring retainable industries. The advantage of focus upon expansion of a small group of industries is that it prevents dissipation of the resources required for entry into a retainable industry. That is, it avoids the situation in which each industry has only a small dribble of resources made available to it, and none of them obtains means sufficient to overcome the costly barriers to entry into a retainable field.

A developing economy, unless it is among the very largest, may not have sufficient resources to provide stimulating tax concessions and infrastructure investments to *many* industries, for that can prevent the outlay from being sufficient to bring success to any one of the industries. Only if the economy confines its efforts and outlays to a small number of retainable industries are enduring successes likely. This seems to have been the approach employed by countries such as Singapore and South Korea when they developed their retainable industries. Our analysis suggests that other developing economies have something useful to learn from their examples.

These difficulties of entry, once overcome in the few industries selected for expansion, will provide a substantial degree of protection against subsequent challenges by other ambitious nations, such as the next low-wage country to develop. But retainability is a double-edged sword. Though the high entry costs provide some protection from competition to an emerging economy that has overcome the entry impediments, it will first have had to overcome the difficulties of entry itself. In this endeavor a developing country can have two important assets: First, it usually has the powerful advantage of low wages. As we saw in chapter 4, an economy has no counter in nonretainable industries to entry by a low-wage country that has attained world productivity limits. But this same observation applies to some of the activities in any industry and can give a developing country entree into some of the activities in a retainable industry. For example, a country can make a start in the high-tech computer industry by using its hard-working and low-paid labor force to assemble electronic components for a company based in an advanced country, while the high-skill processes and designs remain in that firm's home country. This gives the developing country a leg up, but continuation of economic growth will eventually wipe out its wage advantage. It is necessary for the country to follow up its initial foray into the industry with other actions. These may include special government tax advantages granted to firms in the industry, or provision of infrastructure such as shipping facilities and improved utilities, or the requirement that foreign multinational companies make some investment in R&D to accompany production, or even the requirement that the company commit itself to carry out some of its more high-skill operations in the country before it is permitted access to that country's market. Such actions may be able to take the country beyond its early, peripheral role, and its initial entry through low wages can be converted into gradual acquisition of a retainable industry.

5.9 Multinational Corporations and Their Home Countries: A Divergence of Interests

We have just noted the role that multinational firms can play in the gradual acquisition of industries by a developing country. But what is the effect of the activities of a multinational corporation on its home country? Suppose that one of an advanced nation's leading companies decides to build manufacturing capacity in a foreign country. It may do this for any of the reasons just mentioned: that country may offer lower wages with fairly high productivity, newly built infrastructure, special governmental concessions to the company, or access to new markets.

If that new capacity takes the form of a production facility, its establishment may send both knowledge and capital abroad. If the firm has chosen well and can produce cheaply and effectively abroad, the products made there may even end up returning as imports to the firm's own home country. This overseas investment decision may then prove to be very good for that multinational firm. But there remains the question: Is the decision good for its own country? Our analysis indicates that the answer depends on whether the home country is or is not in the zone of conflict relative to its trading partner. If it is in the zone of mutual gain, the buildup of its partner is just what both countries need. Exporting capital and knowledge to another country brings that country closer to the position of an ideal trading partner for the advanced country and benefits both nations. However, if the advanced country is in the zone of conflict, then this export of knowledge and capital just pushes it further from its best, hilltop position. Here the activities of multinational corporations may result in an improvement for the trading partner but it can constitute an actual loss of national income for the company's home country.[7]

The real-world implication is that when a U.S. corporation invests in a less developed country such as Pakistan (or Indonesia or Mauritania), it is likely to be serving the national interests of both its own nation and the less developed country. But when a U.S. company invests in Germany or Japan (relative to which the United States is in the zone of conflict), then the company is probably pursuing its own ends effectively and helping the prosperity of those countries, but its actions may well be detrimental to the U.S. national interest. Mexico appears to be an ambiguous case. These are situations that the United States did not face when it was an isolated economic power. Then it was much more likely that the prosperity of its companies would translate into the prosperity of its people. Although the phrasing is jarring, it was probably true, at least in this arena, that "What is good for our country is good for General Motors, and vice versa."[8] Jobs were created, wages paid, and capital invested in the United States. It is important to realize that, in contrast, in today's world the interests of a company and of its home country in location of production facilities can diverge sharply.

5.10   The Bottom Line: A Nation's Ability to Pay Its Workers High Wages

While we have talked about the importance of creating and retaining industries in terms of an abstraction called national income, we should not forget that behind that abstraction lies a very tangible matter: the wages that a country can pay to its working men and women. To a reasonable approximation, high per-capita national income translates into high wages, low per-capita national income means low wages, and on this hinges the standard of living of a nation's citizens. Raising of living standards is the essential task upon which this book focuses. We have shown that if a nation loses its share of world industries because its productivity lags or for any other reason, national income and the nation's wage-earners are apt to be the ultimate victims.

5.11   Concluding Remark

Free trade is not always and automatically benign. There is much yet to be learned about the implications of national interests in international trade. Nevertheless, the main outlines of what we have sketched here are unlikely to change.[9]

We have shown that there can be inherent conflicts as well as mutual gain for nations engaged in global trade. We have shown that both the conflict and the possibilities for mutual gain follow a systematic pattern. Among developed nations changes that benefit one of them may well come at the expense of the other. But there can also be, up to a certain point, real symbiosis between the enhancement of the real income of a less developed country and that of its more developed trading partner. Both gain if the less affluent country becomes more highly industrialized.

It is here, in the spontaneous partnership between the developed and the much less developed, that sanguine pronouncements about the benefits of trade appear to have their strongest foundation. Here, it is likely to be true that what is good for one trading partner is good for the other. Here, for the developed country, it is likely to be true that in helping its partner develop, it also helps itself. But this is only half of a picture that also has a darker side.

II

For the Specialist: Further Theory and Extensions

6

The Economies Model, the Equilibria, and the Number of Specialized Outcomes

To understand more fully our characterization of the equilibria that emerge from the analysis, it is necessary to lay out our analytical model of international trade, the equilibrium concept that we employed, and the calculation that leads to our conclusion about the vast number of candidate equilibria available to the market mechanism in a world of scale economies. This chapter and the chapters that follow are thus primarily written for specialists in the field.

First, it is important to recognize that our equilibria are not the product of a particularly unorthodox model. Indeed, our model deviates from the classical model of international trade in only one respect: We assume that the production relationships are characterized by scale economies rather than by constant or diminishing returns to scale. The model's basic components are a set of demand functions in each country for the different commodities, and a set of production functions in each country for the different commodities. As in the classical model we define equilibrium as a set of outputs and prices that satisfies the following three requirements: (1) for each commodity the quantity supplied equals quantity demanded, (2) with only one input—labor—the total revenue of each industry is exactly equal to labor cost so that there is zero economic profit,[1] and (3) the labor in each country is fully employed.[2]

Each of these requirements yields a set of equations, which together determine the values of the variables of the model. The variables include the quantity of each good consumed in each of the two countries, the quantity of each good produced in each country, the share of the total world output of each particular good produced in each country, the quantity of labor each country devotes to the production of each commodity, the price of each good, the wage rate in each country, and total income in each country. The model also employs four assumptions: first, that the world is composed of only two countries,[3] second, that there is only a single productive input, labor, third, that the quantity of labor available to each country is a fixed and given quantity, and, fourth, that the demand functions in each country can be integrated into a national utility function of Cobb-Douglas form. As is well known, this last premise implies that in each country the total amount spent on each commodity is fixed and does not vary with the price of the commodity, that is, all demands are unit elastic at all prices and quantities. Then the amount spent on some good I is a fixed fraction of national income, with that fraction given by the exponent of good I consumption in the Cobb-Douglas utility function. These assumptions are adopted to simplify the formal analysis, and we believe that they do not affect our conclusions.

6.1   Perfectly Specialized Outcomes as Stable Equilibria

A perfectly specialized outcome is defined as one in which, for each (and every) commodity I, the share of I that is produced in one of the two countries is zero while the other country's share of world output of that good is unity (100 percent). Our analysis will focus on such perfectly specialized solutions, because (as is well known) scale economies lead the market mechanism toward perfect specialization ("natural monopoly") and also because, as will be seen later (chapter 9), the inclusion of nonspecialized solutions complicates the analysis, but in the end produces the same results.

Intuitively the reason that equilibria will be specialized under scale economies is straightforward. Moreover the same reasoning indicates that these specialized equilibria will be locally stable, meaning that market forces will return the economy to any such equilibrium outcome after something makes the economy deviate slightly from it. For example, in a perfectly specialized equilibrium, widgets will be produced exclusively in only one country, say, France. By virtue of the resulting scale economies that accrue to France, it will then have a substantial advantage over any potential entrant who hopes to embark on widget production incrementally, beginning on a small scale. Such a small-scale entrant will, because of its relatively high costs, be unable to compete against the incumbent, France, and will soon be driven altogether from the field by market forces. Thus the world economy will automatically be pushed back by market forces toward the initial equilibrium in which France was the sole producer of widgets. It is not too difficult to construct a formal dynamic model encompassing this scenario and confirming the sort of stability just described.

So far we have suggested that equilibria under scale economies tend to be perfectly specialized outcomes. However, somewhat more surprising and more important for our analysis is the converse. Each and every perfectly specialized outcome (assignment) is an equilibrium. A proof is easily sketched. It is sufficient to show that any specialized outcome can satisfy all of the three sets of conditions that define an equilibrium. We now do so, in several steps.

1. Determination of expenditure on a good with the given assignment. First, consider any specialized assignment of production among countries in which France is the sole producer of widgets. We test whether this assignment can be an equilibrium of a given model with known demand and production functions. Given the assumed Cobb-Douglas utility function, the share of each country's income that will be spent on every good is known. For the moment, assume that the income of each country is also given. Then the dollar amount that will be spent on widgets (or any other good) in each country is determined directly by multiplying income by share spent on widgets.

2. Zero profit and level of employment in each industry. With this information we can go on to show that the given specialized assignment can, with the equilibrium quantity of labor in each industry, satisfy the first equilibrium requirement: zero profits. At the same time we will see how the equilibrium level of employment of labor in each industry can be determined. Zero profits in the widget industry can be ensured if exactly the amount that consumers spend on widgets, as already determined, is paid to French widget workers, since no other country produces widgets. Hence the zero-profit condition can be satisfied by the given specialized outcome if the number of French widget workers times the French wage rate equals the (given) world expenditure on widgets. For this reason equilibrium employment in any French industry, call it industry I, in the given specialized outcome equals world expenditure on I divided by the French wage rate. So the next step is to find the French wage rate.

3. Full employment and determination of wage rates and national income. Next we turn to the second equilibrium condition: full employment in each country, and determination of the wage rate in each country. We have just seen that with world expenditure on a good given, employment in an industry will vary inversely with the national

wage rate. Therefore the full employment requirement of equilibrium can clearly be satisfied by selecting a wage-rate figure at which the sum of the employment figures for all of the individual industries in which France is a producer in our given assignment equals the total French labor force.[4] That wage rate multiplied by the size of the total French labor force also tells us French national income. Thus for any specialized outcome the zero-profit and the full employment requirements of equilibrium can be satisfied by a unique wage rate and a unique employment figure in every industry.

4. Supply-demand equality and determination of prices. To complete our proof that a specialized outcome is compatible with the requirements of equilibrium, it is left only to show that this is true for the remaining requirement—that quantity supplied equals quantity demanded in each industry. Given the amount of labor employed in each industry, as obtained in the preceding paragraphs, the production function tells us the quantity of each product supplied. With total world expenditure on each product fixed, the quantity demanded varies inversely with the price. That is, quantity of good I demanded must equal the given world expenditure on I divided by the price of I. Hence one can always select a price for I at which the quantity demanded equals the (known) quantity supplied. This completes the argument.

In summary, any perfectly specialized outcome, that is, any preselected assignment of the world's traded commodities specifying which good will be produced in what country (and only in that country), can satisfy the three requirements of an equilibrium at a suitable level of employment in each industry, an appropriate wage rate in each country, and an appropriate price for each good. The level of employment in each industry and the wage rate can ensure zero profit in each industry and full employment in each country, while the price of each good can ensure that the quantity of that item demanded equals the quantity supplied. Thus, given any specialized outcome, market forces will presumably drive prices, wages, and employment level in each industry toward these equilibrium levels. We conclude that every perfectly specialized outcome can, indeed, satisfy the requirements of equilibrium.

We have also seen that those equilibria must all be locally stable— that a small deviation from such an equilibrium (in which one of the countries tries to enter on a small scale[5] an industry from which it was previously absent) cannot persist because the small-scale entrant's cost must then be too high to permit it to compete. This is a result that has previously been described clearly in the literature (e.g., see Krugman and Venables 1992, pp. 4–5).

6.2 Number of Perfectly Specialized Equilibria

The fact that all specialized solutions are equilibria led to the vast number of equilibria, upon which the discussion of chapter 2 of part I focused. It is now easy to determine just how many specialized equilibria there will be in a model with two countries and n different traded goods. This is simply a matter of determining how many specialized assignments of production of the n goods are possible. For each good there are two possible specialized assignments: Widgets can be produced exclusively in France or exclusively in the U.K. Assignment of the task of production of a second good doubles the number of possible outcomes, because for any assignment of the first good there are two possible assignments of the second, yielding 2^2 possible assignments. Continuing in this way, there must be 2^n possible assignments of n goods. If we exclude the two extreme cases in which one of the countries is not assigned any good at all to produce, we are left with a total of $2^n - 2$ possible specialized assignments. This number grows far faster than the number of goods that are traded, with the number of possible equilibria consequently soon reaching enormous levels.

We have thus described the relationships, the variables, and the assumptions that constitute our model. Aside from a few simplifying premises, it differs from the classical trade model only in its scale economies assumption. We have provided a definition of equilibrium and its formal requirements, and have given reasons why, under scale economies, equilibria tend to be perfectly specialized assignments, and why those equilibria tend to have stability properties. We outlined a proof of the theorem that every specialized assignment is an equilibrium. Finally, we demonstrated the central result of this chapter: The scale economies case does, indeed, yield a vast number of perfectly specialized equilibria.

7   Mapping Trade Outcomes: The Shape of the Graph, Beneficial and Harmful Equilibria, and the Role of the Market

In chapter 3 we saw that the shape of the regions formed by the multitude of candidate equilibria for the two trading countries plays a crucial role in our analysis. The hill shape of this region's upper and lower frontiers enables us to determine when a country will gain and when it will lose by success in capturing an industry from its trading partner. The relative position of the peaks of the upper frontiers for the two countries shows the circumstances when the two countries will both gain from the migration of industries from one of the countries to the other, as opposed to those circumstances when their interests are in conflict. The shape of these regions of equilibria, and that of their upper frontiers in particular, show also when a country can be threatened with losses rather than gains from trade and suggests how common or rare this disturbing phenomenon can be. Thus it is important to provide some explanation of how that shape comes about. This chapter begins with such an explanation and then describes the linear program that we use to calculate the boundary from our trade model when we are given the values of the parameters.

7.1   Hill Shape of the Equilibrium Region: An Intuitive Derivation of the Upper Frontier

We will begin with the general shape of only the upper frontiers of the equilibrium regions for the two countries. These are the frontiers from which we obtain most of our conclusions. We again need to refer briefly to a third frontier, the world upper-income frontier, which indicates the upper boundary of the absolute incomes of the two countries combined. This aggregate income frontier shows the highest attainable world income for each point on the horizontal axis, that is, for each value of Z_1, which is the relative income of country 1. The combined

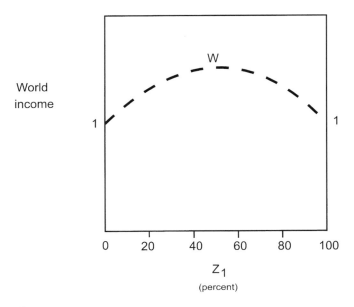

Figure 7.1
World upper income boundary

absolute income of the two countries can be calculated from our equilibrium model for each perfectly specialized assignment just as easily and in the same manner as for the aggregated income for a single country, and is shown as the dashed curve in figure 7.1.

This frontier is dome shaped. We see this in all our more than one hundred calculated models. There are two reasons for this. First the world's upper income frontier can be expected to be lower as we get near either end of the curve because at such at those extremes the entire labor force of one of the two countries is working on the very few goods that remain to that country. If we assume diminishing marginal rate of substitution among the world's products, the resulting large output quantities of those few items add much less value to the total world output than if that country's labor force were divided among a much larger share of the world's industries, as occurs in the middle of the graph. That is, near the edges of the curve there must be such an abundance of these few products that their total market value will be relatively low—much lower than the sum of the added values that could be obtained by moving much of that country's overspecialized labor force to a multitude of other industries. The second is to be found in the Ricardian explanation that output gains from trade result from specialization and the consequent opportunities to exercise comparative advantage. We recall that at both the right-hand and left-hand ends of our basic graph (see, e.g., figure 7.2 or figure 7.3), there will be no trade because at these extremes all traded goods are produced exclusively by a single country. That is, the right-hand end of the graph represents a tradeless state of autarky for country 1, in which it produces all n goods for itself. Similarly the left-hand end of the graph is a state of autarky for country 2. However, as we move toward the center of the diagram, the industries are divided ever more evenly between the two countries, until at a point near the middle (i.e., near $Z_1 = 0.5$) the two countries are each the exclusive producer of about the same number of commodities. Now, as is recognized by anyone who has studied international trade, this means that if the production functions of the two countries differ, then the potential Ricardian gains from trade will be increased as the industries are divided up between the countries. So, if there are productivity gains from trade, at all values of Z_1 intermediate between zero and unity, the height of the world's combined income frontier will be higher than it is at either of its end points. If there is some most efficient assignment of goods to producer countries, then there will be some point, call it W, in the interior of the diagram at which the world income frontier reaches its maximum. All of this means that the dashed world income frontier in figure 7.1 can be assumed to be dome shaped.

From this world income frontier we can now readily find the upper-income frontiers of the individual countries. Since country 1's income at any equilibrium point is total world income, $W(Z_1)$, multiplied by Z_1, country 1's share, that is, $Z_1W(Z_1)$, its upper-income frontier will be dome shaped (the curve containing point M_1 in figure 7.2).[1] Its height, $0W(0)$, must be zero at the left-hand end of the graph where Z_1, country 1's share of world income, is zero. Similarly, at its right-hand end, where country 1's share is 100 percent, the height of country 1's upper frontier must be the same as that of the world income frontier. Thus, if the world frontier has the general shape depicted, the upper-income frontier of country 1 must also have the shape shown in the graph. It too will be a hill, with its peak, point M_1, to the right of that of W because at W world income is level, but country 1's *share* is increasing. The upper income frontier of country 2, the income of $(1 - Z_1)W(Z_1)$, will have the same general shape, roughly the mirror image of that of country 1. Thus the upper income frontier of country 2 will also be

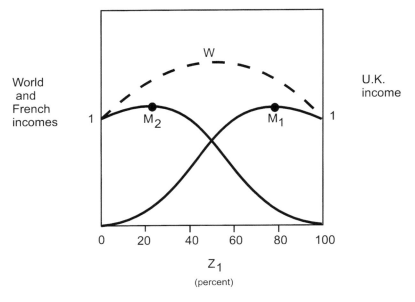

Figure 7.2
Three upper income boundaries

roughly hill shaped, with its peak, point M_2, to the left of W and, hence, to the left of the peak, M_1, of country 1's frontier. All of this is depicted in figure 7.2, where we see that as we move to the right (so that country 1's share of world income rises steadily), the country 1 frontier can be taken to move steadily ever closer to the world frontier, approaching the latter asymptotically. This completes the intuitive derivation of the shape of the upper-income frontiers of the two countries, on which the bulk of our policy discussion depends.[2]

7.2 Region of Candidate Equilibria:
How the Boundaries Are Found

As has just been said, much of our analysis depends crucially on the shape of the region of candidate equilibria, a configuration that is characterized by its boundaries. It is consequently important for us to describe how those boundaries can be calculated, to assure the reader that they are determined in a defensible manner and that they do indeed characterize the equilibrium region accurately.

First, how do we know that these boundaries exist? We can safely assume, given the finite resources available to any economy, that the level of national income offered by any equilibrium is also finite. Moreover the formula for the number of perfectly specialized equilibria described in the previous chapter shows that while that number grows very large as the number of traded commodities increases, with any given set of commodities that number is still clearly finite. Thus for any given share of world income, Z, obtained by one of the two countries (i.e., for any given position on the horizontal axis in our graph), if there are any equilibrium points directly above that position, there must be one such point that is the highest in that set of points, and its height too must be finite. In other words, the set of candidate equilibrium points must be bounded from above at every point, Z, on the horizontal axis. Since national income must also be nonnegative, these points must also be bounded from below. The conclusion follows: Both an upper and a lower boundary for the set of equilibrium points must exist. The next problem is to find each of these frontiers.

Before describing how this is done, we want to point out again that we are carrying out our analysis at present considering only the perfectly specialized equilibria. There do exist nonspecialized equilibria too. Indeed, the real world provides us virtually with only nonspecialized equilibria—assignments of goods to countries in which most goods are produced by more than one country, though most of these, plausibly, are unstable in a world of scale economies. Later we will come back to the nonspecialized equilibria and their relation to the region of perfectly specialized equilibria.

But for now, returning to the central issue, it should be plausible that the calculation of the boundaries of the equilibrium region is a matter of mathematical programing. To find the upper frontier, we must find the equilibrium point that maximizes the national income (or that maximizes the total utility if the total utility function is known) of the county in question, for any given value of Z, subject to the constraints that ensure that the equilibrium points considered satisfy the sets of equations that constitute the basic requirements of equilibrium. As we saw in the previous chapter, these three requirements are full employment in each country, quantity of each commodity supplied equals quantity demanded, and zero profit in each industry. We can formulate a mathematical program whose constraints are these three sets of equations,[3] and whose maximum is either the total utility or the national income of the country in question. The solution to this program constitutes the point on our upper frontier corresponding to any given point Z on the horizontal axis, and repetition of this calculation for each and every value of Z yields the entire upper frontier. Similarly, for a given value of Z, we can calculate the minimum value of national income (subject to the same three constraints) and then repeat the calculation for different values of Z. This procedure traces out the lower frontier of the region of perfectly specialized equilibria. That, in principle, is how the upper and lower frontiers of the equilibrium region are determined.

7.3   Two Complications of the Boundary Determination

This description of the boundary-setting process may seem too easy. In reality there are at least two complications, as well as two simplifications, that we must describe.

First, we must list the variables whose values the programming calculation is to determine. The variables of the model include the prices of the goods produced, the quantity of each good consumed in each country, the quantity of labor assigned to its production, the wage rate in each country and the share of world output of each commodity that is produced in each country. This last variable plays a key role in our analysis because it is this variable that describes the assignments of production. We call this variable $x_{i,j}$, which denotes the share of world output of good I that, in the assignment in question, is produced in country J. In a perfectly specialized assignment $x_{i,j}$ is equal to 1 if country J is the producer of good I; and $x_{i,j}$ equals zero if country J is not its producer. Clearly, if we know the values of all of these variables, then we know exactly to which country the production of each good is assigned. In other words, each possible assignment is described by the set of zero and one values of the $x_{i,j}$ variables.

Next, we will see that this is all one needs to know to locate a perfectly specialized equilibrium on our graph of outcomes. This is because, as we saw in the previous chapter, for any given assignment the equilibrium conditions can be used to determine the value of every remaining variable. The zero-profit conditions determine how much labor will be employed in an industry, the full employment condition in each country then determines its wage rate, and so on. Thus our mathematical programming problem of boundary drawing does not have to be burdened with calculation of the values of other variables. It need merely determine the value of each $x_{i,j}$ variable, and calculation of the others can be postponed. The key role of the $x_{i,j}$ variables is the first of the complications that affects the mathematical programming calculation of the upper- and lower-income frontiers—the boundaries of the region of perfectly specialized equilibria.

The second complication arises from the fact that in a perfectly specialized equilibrium the $x_{i,j}$ variables must be integers, either zero or unity, and hence discontinuous. This poses a problem that can be solved by either of two approaches. One can turn to the methods of integer programming, using this form of mathematical programming to determine the maxima and minima. This complicates the calculation somewhat, and it yields boundaries that are not very smooth because of the gaps that the finite number of perfectly specialized equilibrium points must inevitably leave in the graph. The alternative approach is simply, during this programming calculation, to ignore the requirement that the $x_{i,j}$ variables have only integer values and to assume implicitly that the variables are continuous. It can be proved that when the number of traded commodities is relatively large, the two methods of calculation yield boundaries that are very close to one another.

7.4   Two Simplifications of the Boundary-Drawing Process

Without attempting a detailed explanation, it should be noted that the preceding description of the method of determining the upper and lower boundaries also makes the process seem more complex than it turns out to be. This is because, first, the required calculation entails a mathematical program with only a single constraint, and second, the program is linear—with all of the simplifications that result.

The elimination of all but one of the equilibrium requirements is permitted by our focus upon just the one set of variables, the $x_{i,j}$. By postponing the calculation of the other variables such as wages and prices, we are permitted to ignore temporarily the equilibrium equations that will be used to determine the values of those variables. With these equilibrium requirements out of the way, we need only determine the values of the $x_{i,j}$ variables that maximize the national income of the country in question, given the value of Z (the relative national income of that country). For this we need only one constraint: the equation that determines the country's national income as a function of the $x_{i,j}$ and Z.

That equation is straightforward. With unit price elasticity of demand for each good in each country, as our model assumes, the value of Z determines (relative) world expenditure on each commodity I. The amount of income our country receives from production of good I is then this fixed expenditure multiplied by $x_{i,j}$, its share of the world's output of I. That country's total income then is the sum of these amounts, that is, the sum for all goods I, of world expenditure on I multiplied by $x_{i,j}$.

Thus we end up with only one constraint. This constraint is clearly linear in the variables whose values are to be determined, the $x_{i,j}$. Our calculation for the upper frontier, for any given value of Z, then amounts to the one-constraint linear program in which the maximand is the national income of country J and whose constraint is the linear equation that has just been described. The entire upper frontier is then calculated by repeating this calculation for the range of Z values.

The lower frontier is patently calculated similarly, only this time by minimization of country J's national income subject to the same constraint.

7.5   On Tightness of the Boundaries

How accurately do the boundaries calculated in this manner describe the set of equilibria? The answer is that when the number of traded commodities is small, the boundaries so calculated unavoidably leave much to be desired. If the world trades in only two goods, widgets and gidgets, there are only four specialized assignments: the one in which the U.K. produces both, the one in which France produces both, the one in which France produces all the widgets and the U.K. all the gidgets, and the one in which widget and gidget production are switched. Any set of boundaries for all levels of Z must then encompass a great deal of empty space when there are only two traded goods. But, as the number of traded commodities increases, the boundaries rapidly begin to do a much better job of representing the equilibrium points, and, as our graphs in earlier chapters clearly show, by the time the number of goods exceeds ten or so, their correspondence seems quite acceptable. Indeed, we have a result considerably stronger than that. For it is possible to prove:

THEOREM 1   (Filling-in theorem) If one selects any arbitrary point on the boundary and the number of traded goods considered in the model increases, there will be a number of goods beyond which an equilibrium point will lie "right next to" the selected boundary point.

That is, if we preselect any standard of closeness (the distance between the two points should be less than some number r), then, for a number of goods sufficiently large, there will be an equilibrium point whose distance to our selected boundary point is less than r. In sum, with the number of traded goods very large the boundaries calculated by the methods just described must fit the set of equilibrium points very snugly.[4]

7.6   Observations on Imperfectly Specialized Equilibria and the Two Boundaries

We deal next with an issue that is always just below the surface in our analysis of the shape of the equilibrium region and its boundaries. In working on this matter, we focus persistently on the perfectly specialized equilibria in order to facilitate out determination of the properties of the equilibrium region and to calculate its boundaries. However, the real world is characterized by equilibria that are not perfectly specialized, though the number of countries in which the more sophisticated and more high-tech commodities are produced is often fairly small. The natural question is whether the region that we have shown to contain all the perfectly specialized equilibria, and that tends to "fill up" with perfectly specialized equilibrium points, also contains the nonspecialized equilibria. Here we will merely report the answer, without attempting to describe the proof. It can be shown that:

THEOREM 2   The upper boundary is a ceiling over all equilibria.

If we were to calculate an upper boundary of all equilibria as we have done for only the perfectly specialized ones, we would obtain the same curve. This reflects the fact that all the nonspecialized equilibria lie under the upper boundary of the specialized equilibria, and that they also press right up against the upper boundary as the number of equilibria increases.

The place where the region of nonspecialized equilibria does depart from the region of specialized equilibria is in its lower boundary. As common sense indicates, it is possible in the presence of economies of scale to get worse outcomes by dividing industries (as happens in nonspecialized equilibria), and thus losing economies of scale, than from only specialized outcomes. Consequently there can be nonspecialized equilibria below the lower boundary of the region of specialized equilibria. How many there are, and how far below that lower boundary they occur, depends on the strength of the economies of scale.

In one specially interesting case, when the economies of scale have been exhausted at the level of production actually attained in the industries so that the production curves have become linear, the nonspecialized equilibria will all lie within the region of specialized equilibria.

The general situation is illustrated in figure 7.3, where the light grey points represent unspecialized equilibria, all calculated by computer from a particular concrete model. We see that there are, indeed, such points below the lower-income frontier.

Yet this is not the end of the story. While the region we have analyzed does not generally contain all pertinent equilibrium points, in cases where the number of traded commodities is fairly large, that region does contain all (or virtually all) of the equilibria that matter. That is, it tends to contain all of the stable equilibria, thus omitting only those that are apt to be highly transitory. There are two reasons for this.

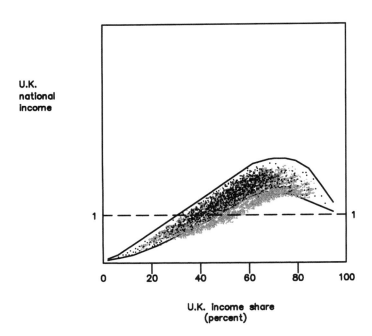

Figure 7.3
Inclusion of unspecialized equilibria

First, if economies of scale are substantial, there are strong forces working against the stability of any unspecialized equilibrium. Consider an equilibrium in which good I is produced simultaneously in two countries, A and B. Then equilibrium requires that the marginal cost of the product in the two countries be equal, for otherwise one of the countries could underprice the other and expand its market share of product I, thereby modifying the initial assignment and causing the economy to leave the initial point. But, even if the marginal cost of good I is the same in both countries, any fortuitous increase in sales by country A must reduce its marginal cost below that of B, thereby making possible a further rise in A's sales of good I, further reducing its marginal costs, and so on, until the production of I becomes perfectly specialized, with all of it being produced by A. It is even possible to show that if there is more than one shared industry, stability is not attainable if scale economies are substantial. If there is only one industry shared by several countries, however, there is a flaw in the instability argument. As a country acquires more of an industry, its wage will tend to be driven upward, and that constitutes an offset to the cost reduction that scale economies provide in the wake of the output expansion. One may well judge that the countervailing power of the wage rise is virtually certain to be weak in a model with many traded commodities, since expansion in the output of only one of the country's large number of products is unlikely to have much of an effect on the country's wage rate, though this expansion can cut the cost of that one industry significantly as a result of its scale economies. It is plausible that the weak force of the wage increase will not be overwhelmed by the cost reduction contributed by scale economies if those scale economies come to an end beyond some level of output. Then after some point the production functions become nearly linear.

In reality the erosion of scale economies beyond some level of output seems quite common, and this explains the patent stability and frequency of shared-industry assignments. Fortunately, when production functions are linear or near linear after a certain point, the shared equilibrium points will all lie inside (in the linear case) or almost inside (in the almost-linear case) the region of equilibria.

We can conclude that while the space between the upper- and lower-income frontiers does not contain all of the nonspecialized equilibria, that space can quite justifiably be characterized as a close approximation to the region of stable equilibria.

7.7   Poor Welfare Performance and Inefficiency of Some Equilibria

We saw in chapter 3 that many of the locally stable equilibria that arise in a scale economies model can be damaging to the interests of one of the trading countries. We learned that there exist many equilibria near either vertical axis of the graph at which both countries are worse off and possibly very much worse off than they would be at equilibria closer to the center of the diagram. In other words, the analysis indicates that under scale economies the invisible hand can blunder; it can sustain an equilibrium point that is locally stable and yet does not enjoy the beneficial welfare properties that the economics literature associates with the market mechanism, at least in a regime of perfect competition. We will presently consider explicitly why the market mechanism can lose some of its benign powers in a world of scale economies. First, however, we offer a brief and simple proof that equilibria of the scale-economies model need not even satisfy the requirements of productive efficiency (defined in the usual way to mean that productive efficiency yields the largest possible output of any given commodity that is achievable without any offsetting reduction in the output of any other commodity).

The discussion is framed in terms of Ricardo's two countries, England and Portugal, but substituting for his cloth and wine two contemporary products, computers and Walkman radios, in whose production we may expect scale economies. In such a two-good, two-country model it must be remembered that there are always exactly two perfectly specialized assignments. Portugal can produce all the Walkmans and England all the computers, or the reverse can be true.

In figure 7.4 curves PP' and EE' are the production frontiers for Portugal and England. Here the convexity (downward) of the two frontiers represents the presence of scale economies because toward the center of the frontier, where the countries' production is unspecialized and the output of each good is relatively small, the output vector is held down (the output point is closer to the origin than it would be in the linear case).[5] The two specialized solutions are $S' = (E', P)$ and $S = (P', E)$. In the first of these England produces all the world's Walkmans and Portugal produces all of the computers, while in the second of these the production assignment is reversed. Both of these solutions are obviously locally stable equilibria at prices that clear the markets, because if either country tries to produce a small quantity of the other's

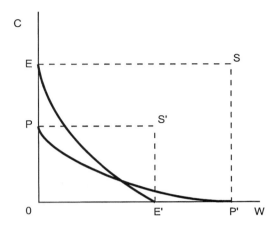

Figure 7.4
Inefficiency of some specialized equilibria

product it will fail because of its high costs. Yet, as shown in figure 7.4, where the two frontiers intersect, the one specialized point S clearly dominates the other, S', so the latter must be inefficient. This must always be so where the two countries' production frontiers have an odd number of intersections because then one country must be able to produce a maximum of more Walkmans than the other, and the other country must then be able to produce more computers than the first. Hence the specialized equilibrium in which the first country produces all the Walkmans and the second country produces all the computers must then dominate the equilibrium in which the assignment of commodity production to the two countries is reversed. This example clearly shows that:

THEOREM 3   (Existence of inefficient equilibria) In a world of scale economies, stable equilibria can be inefficient.

Numerical examples are clearly not difficult to construct.

7.8   Why the Market Cannot Generally Prevent Equilibria with Poor Welfare Properties

One could well ask why the market mechanism does not automatically eliminate those equilibria of the model that are decidedly inferior in their welfare performance. That is, suppose equilibrium B offers both trading countries higher incomes or even larger quantities of all commodities than another equilibrium A. Why don't entrepreneurs in both countries recognize the shareable profit opportunities that are available if the world economy is initially at A, and why do they not act so as to move the world to B? Alternatively, why does not arbitrage enable the market to do the welfare-maximizing job we expect of it in a world of universally diminishing returns? The realistic answer is that in practice business managers neither are aware of the identity of the distant opportunities that are really promising, nor do they know how to get to that better equilibrium. Getting to B requires entrepreneurs in each country to select among the vast array of goods that they may never have produced before. Neither previous experience nor any other market signal will make these possibilities, much less the best or even the viable choices, obvious in advance. Moreover the investments required for the move from A to B are not only very risky—they must also be very large, since entry into the requisite industries on a small scale is doomed to failure. In such circumstances one could surely expect no automatic forces to move the economy from A to B. The risks of the necessary investments are too great, and the available information too sparse to ensure that such welfare-enhancing moves will generally be carried out by market forces. Anyone with any experience in business or government is surely aware that no one knows which, if any, equilibrium points at a distance from the current assignment guarantee mutual gains to the trading nations involved or even higher profits or a higher national income to either country alone. With such great gaps in the pertinent information, great risks, and high outlays required for the move, how can one expect arbitrage or any other instrument of the market mechanism to move the economy from an undesirable equilibrium point? Even a country stuck in an equilibrium that is worse for it than autarky is surely kept there by ignorance. This is simply because autarky is a state of affairs that it has never experienced and that it has no way of evaluating. Thus, though a country might benefit by simply closing its borders to all imports of goods whose production is characterized by scale economies, the prospect must be a frightening leap into the unknown.

Another reason, perhaps more fundamental, prevents the market mechanism from carrying out such improving moves from one equilibrium to another. Market signals are entirely local. They tell the business managers only about the partial derivatives of profit that small moves from an initial position will yield. When there is a profusion of local maxima, a move that brings one higher on the current profit hill does not offer any information about other faraway hills whose peaks may be much higher than that of the current hillock. A move toward the summit of the current hill can easily bring one farther away from a far higher peak of a distant hill. In sum, in a world of scale economies market forces can be relied on to drive the economy toward a local maximum of profits and even of welfare. But these forces have no power to free the world economy from that local optimum and move it toward one that is unambiguously better. That is why, under scale economies, decidedly inferior equilibria can nevertheless be locally stable. The invisible hand can indeed, by the happenstance of history, find itself stuck at an equilibrium that is locally optimal but globally far inferior to others, even inferior to the autarky equilibrium for at least one of the trading countries.

7.9   Concluding Comment

While, in practice, the calculation of the boundaries of the region of perfectly specialized equilibria involves complications in the requisite computer programs, the logic of the process is not difficult. We have seen how boundaries can be computed by a simple linear programming exercise. We have seen that the region between the two frontiers characterizes the perfectly specialized equilibria, since it contains all of them, and since the equilibrium points tend to fill up the region as the number of traded commodities in the model grows. Finally, we have seen that while unspecialized equilibria can lie below this region (but never above it), the nonspecialized points that are not inside or close to the region tend to be unstable. In other words, in a world of scale economies all stable equilibria tend to lie inside the region. In the next chapter we will see that there is a corresponding result for a world of constant returns to scale—a result that offers significant additional insights of its own.

We have also seen from the shape of the region of equilibria that some of the locally stable equilibria will keep the absolute incomes of one of the two countries, and in many cases those of both countries, below their maximal attainable levels. In addition it has been shown that the equilibria can be inefficient. Yet, as we have explained, in our scale economies world the market mechanism loses its ability to move the economy automatically to a superior equilibrium. This is a consequence of the likelihood that the superior equilibria will be located in a relatively distant portion of the region, meaning that entrepreneurs may not be aware of the existence of the opportunities they offer and have may have little idea of the means that can move the economy there. The values of the observable economic parameters provide only local information and offer no guidance on the direction in which the true global optimum lies, or even on the location of equilibria markedly superior to the economy's current position.

8 Conflicting National Interests in Linear Trade Models

This chapter extends our analysis of chapter 4, indicating more of the foundation of the analysis of productivity growth in the classical linear model of international trade.[1] Economists have long understood that a unilateral productivity increase usually contributes to the welfare of the country whose productivity has risen. But the effects on the welfare of the other country—for example, was the U.K. benefited or hurt by the nineteenth-century increase in German steel productivity?—were unclear (and disputed) until the some fairly recent ground-breaking work, including that of Hicks (1953), Dornbusch, Fisher, and Samuelson (1977), Krugman (1979), and that of Stafford and his associates (see Johnson and Stafford 1993 and 1995; Hymans and Stafford 1995). Our analysis confirms their results, showing that such a one-sided productivity improvement can harm a country's trading partner if it enables the one with enhanced productivity in a particular good to increase its share of the two countries' total output of that good, or even to take over the production of that item altogether. But we will take the discussion further and generalize it considerably by relating it to the case of scale economies or the case of high entry costs, where means other than increased productivity, including various forms of government intervention, can be used by one country to acquire an industry from another. We will show, by studying the formal correspondence between linear models and scale economies models, that such a transfer of an industry from one country to another will generally (but not always) benefit the acquiring country at the expense of the other. Our analysis will have direct implications for the design of a nation's trade policy.

It is not much of an oversimplification to say that the classical model of international trade rests on an implicit assumption of universal constant returns to scale, except in the use of land, to which the law of diminishing returns applies. The central theme of this chapter is that much of the story revealed by our analysis of the scale economies case does carry over to situations where there are neither economies nor diseconomies of scale.[2] Our examination of this classical linear case will also offer some additional insights:

1. On the assumption that there is in any industry a maximal level of (labor) productivity attainable by a producer (given the current state of technological knowledge), one obtains a region of equilibria for families of linear models of the sort found for a world of scale economies. Here a family consists of a set of linear models identical in structure and parameter values, except that their productivity coefficients differ from one model to another. As in the case of scale economies, there exist both upper and a lower boundaries for this region that can be approximated closely with the aid of linear programming.

2. Any perfectly specialized solution, in which any good is produced in only one country, will be the equilibrium of some suitably selected linear model. These equilibria can usefully be subdivided into those where a country has attained maximal productivity in each good it produces and those where it has not. In the latter case, increases in the productivity of the producing nation will benefit both trading partners. However, when one of the countries' equilibria entails maximal productivity, then it can be harmed by increases in the productivity of the other country in an industry currently supplied exclusively by the maximal-productivity country, since the improving country may then be able to take the industry away from the current producer.

3. It is possible to determine from the point of view of one of the countries, J, the attributes of the other country that will best serve J's interests. This set of attributes will be said to constitute J's "ideal trading partner." In a broad class of cases, to be the ideal trading partner of country J that partner must be relatively impoverished, characterized by wages less than one-third as high as those in J.

4. The low relative wage that characterizes the ideal trading partner implies that it pays an industrial country, in terms of just its own self-interest, to help its trading partner improve its relative economic position only if that partner's prevailing wage is very low—generally something less than one-third of its own, as just noted. If its trading partner's relative wage is above that low threshold level, the wealthy economy can enhance its economic welfare only through developments

that lead to a decline in the relative wage of its trading partner. This epitomizes the inherent conflict of the interests in the trade of two countries of similar economic status. Once again we see in the linear model the same conflicts of national interests as in the model we discussed earlier involving economies of scale.

8.1 Multiple Equilibria in Linear Models: An Intertemporal Interpretation

The idea that there can be a region of equilibria for linear models may at first seem more than a bit odd. There are good grounds for the standard presumption that a linear model of international trade will usually yield only a single stable equilibrium rather than the thousands or millions of candidate equilibria that we have shown to characterize the scale economies case, and that together constitute the equilibrium region. This is correct, and we will, indeed, deal with models with the unique equilibria to be expected in the linear case. However, as already noted, rather than studying just a single linear model we will, instead, examine entire families of such linear models that are all the same in every respect but one. One model will differ from another in that in the first model the average productivity of labor in country J in the production of good I will be different from the corresponding productivity level in the second model. Each such model will then yield a different equilibrium, and we will focus on the set of equilibria corresponding to one entire family of models—one equilibrium per model. This is in contrast with our scale economies analysis, where all of the equilibria in the equilibrium region are possible outcomes of a single model.

This focus on families of linear models enables us to examine the consequences of growth in the productivity of a country's trading partner. Each linear model in such a family serves as a still picture, a single frame in a motion picture of growth. This will permit us to analyze explicitly the effect on the economic welfare of one country that is caused by growth in the productivity of its trading partner.

8.2 The Graph in the Linear Model

We turn now to our equilibrium-region graph for the case of constant returns to scale, where the production function is assumed to take a particularly simple form. It is assumed that the quantity of good I produced in country J is equal to the quantity of labor $l_{i,j}$ used by the Ith industry in country J multiplied by a constant $e_{i,j}$, which is the (average and marginal) productivity of country J labor in the production of good I. We assume that each of these productivity numbers has some upper bound, the maximal productivity level, for which we use the symbol $e_{i,j\max}$. The productivity of country J labor in industry I cannot currently exceed this amount.

As in the scale economies case, we have seen in chapter 4 that the equilibrium point derived from such a model can be represented by two dots in our, by now, familiar graph (see, e.g., points U_b and F_b in figure 3.5, page 37) one dot for each of the two countries. To obtain the many equilibrium points, we produce a family of linear models by just varying the productivity numbers. That is, suppose that we start off with any linear model given by the three equilibrium requirements described in chapter 7. Then change any or all of the productivity numbers, leaving everything else absolutely unchanged. The result will be two equilibria, the old and the new, which will be said correspondingly to be in the same family of equilibria.

A family of linear models will yield a set of equilibria for each country, each represented by a point in a region of the graph. The region of a country's equilibrium points is, as before, bounded from above, and this upper boundary, the upper national income frontier for the country in question, can be approximated by essentially the same calculation as in the scale economies case. For every Z, one determines the equilibrium that yields the highest absolute national income, subject to the requirements that the output share numbers for each good and each country are consistent with the definition of the country's national income. This is clearly a verbal description of a linear program, and it is exactly the program that was used to determine the upper frontier for scale economies models (chapter 7).

From among such a family of models and their equilibria we can select a smaller set of equilibria that we call maximal-productivity equilibria. These represent all the equilibria yielded by linear models in the selected family in which each country has developed skills sufficient to attain maximal productivity in each of those industries in which it is a producer. These maximal-productivity equilibria are extremely numerous and all lie in a subregion of the region that contains all of the equilibria for the family. We call this the maximal-productivity subregion. As in the scale economies case, this region tends to fill up with equilibrium points as the number of commodities in the model grows.

The maximal productivity subregion is important because it is here that we obtain the relationship between the $2^n - 2$ specialized equilibria of a given scale economies model and a set of the equilibria of the given family of linear models. As we will see in the following section, the relationship goes both ways. Suppose that we select any family of linear models and any one scale economies model then, first, if we calculate all the perfectly specialized equilibria for the scale economies model, we will find $2^n - 2$ corresponding equilibria among the set of maximal productivity equilibria for the given family subject to some straightforward conditions about the models and the equilibrium points, which will be described in the next section. That is, every equilibrium point in the set of specialized equilibrium points for the scale economies model will also be a (specialized equilibrium) point in the maximal-productivity subregion for the selected family of linear models. Second, starting from any set of $2^n - 2$ specialized equilibrium points in the maximal productivity subregion for the given family of linear models, provided that these points satisfy the obviously relevant precondition to be described in the next section, we can (easily) construct a scale economies model with the same specialized equilibrium points.

The subregion of maximal productivity equilibria for the family of linear models in question also is bounded from below, by another curve, the lower national income frontier of country J. This lower boundary is obtained by minimizing for each value of Z the national income in the linear program just described. The two frontier curves are, once more, always roughly hill shaped, and they encompass a crescent-shaped region of equilibria. As is familiar from the scale economies discussion in earlier chapters, for country 1 that region starts off at the bottom of the graph, that is, at the zero point. As we move to the right in the graph, the region always begins to move uphill until it finally reaches a peak, and then it begins to descend again and reaches a point on the right-hand axis of the graph. This point is higher than zero and represents the level of absolute income country 1 would obtain in autarky if all of its industries were to achieve maximal productivity. The reasons for this shape are exactly the same as in the scale economies case: As one moves from left to right in the graph, the world's industries tend largely to migrate into the hands of country 1. But moving ever rightward, country 1 acquires more and more of those industries. Up to a point the resulting increased division of labor between countries enhances world output. Thus, as the size of the world output "pie" grows, country 1's share of the pie simultaneously increases and country 1's welfare must rise—its upper national income frontier moves upward. Ultimately, however, too far a move to the right means that an inefficiently excessive share of the world's industries has been acquired by country 1, cutting total world production so much that country 1 must finally experience declining real income despite its rising share of that shrinking world pie.

The similarity of the shapes of the graphs for the linear models with that for the scale economies case extends also to the location of the peaks of the upper income frontiers. We again have the result that the peak of the frontier for country 1 (whose relative income, Z_1, one reads from left to right) will always lie to the right of the peak for country 2. This again shows the conflict in the interests of the two countries: A value of Z that permits one country to maximize its utility will always force the other country to a utility level well below the latter's maximum.

8.3   Differences between Two-Industry and Many-Industry Models

The conclusions that we have reached in studying linear models with trade in many products seem different, intuitively, from what one is led to expect from the more familiar two-industry models. It turns out that the number of industries does matter. The results we have just described are valid for models with a larger number of industries, usually six or more. Such large models turn out to be significantly different from small models, such as the familiar England–Portugal, wine–textile example.

To get at the reasons for the difference, let us consider that famous example. In that two-industry model the outcome in which Portugal specializes in wine and attains its maximal productivity, and England specializes in textiles and attains its maximal productivity, is best for both countries. It remains the best even when we consider, as we do, all the equilibria attained when productivities are lowered. This contrasts with our usual result, in which the outcome best for one country is a poor one for the other.

It turns out that the large models differ from the small ones in two significant ways: (1) large models do not have the extreme lumpiness of a two-industry model. In large models one country can capture a relatively small industry from the other and benefit from the improved terms of trade without a huge effect on world production, and (2) in large models there will usually be some industries in which neither country has an overwhelming natural advantage.

To see the role of the first of these difference without using an extensive analytical apparatus, let us consider the wine–textile example and simplify things by assuming that the demand for wine and textiles in both countries is the same, that both countries are of the same size, and that each will spend half its national income on wine and half on textiles—a special case of Cobb-Douglas demand.

If both countries are at their maximal productivities, with England much more productive at textiles and Portugal much more productive at wine, the outcome in which each specializes in the industry in which its absolute productivity is greatest is an equilibrium. At this equilibrium each country captures half of world income. Our experience with larger models leads us to consider whether England would gain from a move to an equilibrium in which it obtains more than half of world output. Would England be better off in an equilibrium in which it obtains 55 percent of world output, for example? Let us consider this possibility.

Since England receives all the textile income already, to reach 55 percent of the total it must capture 10 percent of the world's wine revenue. For this to be an equilibrium outcome, England must become competitive in wine. Since England is assumed already to have attained its maximum wine productivity, such competitiveness requires Portugal's productivity to fall close to England's. Since England and Portugal both spend half of their national income on wine, this reduced productivity in the wine industry yields much less wine both for England and for Portugal. There is an equilibrium at which England does get 55 percent of world income, but world output of wine, which was half of world output value, is dramatically decreased. England gets that small increased share, but calculations using this model confirm that the outcome is bad both for England and for Portugal.

However, if we replace the single wine industry with ten smaller Portuguese industries, the result generally is entirely different. We can assign each of these replacement industries exactly the same productivity advantage that Portugal in the previous example had in wine, and we can give the ten together the same total revenue as the single wine industry had. If these industries are all of the same size, then England needs to capture only one of them to get its additional 5 percent of world expenditure.

In this new setting there can be a new equilibrium in which Portugal has undergone a reduction in its productivity in one of the ten industries. In this new competitive equilibrium England is the sole producer in that industry, while Portugal remains the producer with unchanged productivity in the other nine. England now has 55 percent of world income but without the large damaging effect on world output that there was before. Productivity has gone down only in the small industry newly acquired by England and this represents only 5 percent of world income. This contrasts with the effect of reduced productivity in the single huge wine industry. Actual calculations then show that this new equilibrium is better than its predecessor for England and worse for Portugal. For England its share increase more than counterbalances the much reduced effect on world productivity.

A second difference between the two-product and many-product cases is attributable to the existence in the latter of some industries in which productivity differences are large, and some in which they are small. In today's world there are many industries in which acquirable knowledge and skill matter more than any inherent natural advantage. In contrast with industries in which one or the other country has major natural advantages, such as very favorable climate or abundant raw materials, productivity in such industries is not very different in different countries. These provide a pool of industries that can more easily be taken over by a country in moving from one equilibrium to another equilibrium at which it has a greater income share. Such a move can be carried out with relatively little loss in world output and so benefit the industry-acquiring country while harming the other. We sometimes refer to these industries as "swing" industries.

In such a takeover the increased share effect is present, but the productivity effect, the loss of world output when the takeover occurs, tends to be much smaller than it would have been had productivities in the taken-over industries differed sharply between countries. Again, this is an effect that simply may not be present in two-industry models. In the wine–textile example England has an advantage in textiles and Portugal in wine. There are no other industries, so there cannot exist any intermediate industries, those in which neither country has a substantial productivity advantage.

These two differences explain why in two-industry models there is likely to be an equilibrium such that any movement from it will harm both countries, while in a many-industry model such a move will benefit one country at the expense of the other. In the latter case it is easier for a country to obtain a larger share of the world output pie without causing the pie to shrink substantially.

8.4   Correspondence Theorems

The qualitative similarity between the regions of equilibria in the linear and the scale economies cases derives from a correspondence (to which we turn next) between the equilibria and their regions for the two cases. This correspondence was described very roughly in the preceding section. From any given equilibrium of a scale economies model, one can construct a linear model with a directly corresponding equilibrium, meaning that the two equilibria have the same income-share values, Z_j, as well as the same output shares for each good in each country, and the same average productivity of labor, at the given output, for any good actually produced in country J. Specifically, it is possible to prove:

CORRESPONDENCE THEOREM 1   One can find the linear model in a given family that yields a maximal-productivity equilibrium corresponding directly to a particular scale economies equilibrium.

The linear model is found simply by taking the scale-economies production functions $f_{i,j}(l_{i,j})$, calculating from them the average productivity figure, $f_{i,j}(l_{i,j})/l_{i,j}$, for each good I produced in country J and then, in the family of linear models, setting the corresponding productivity parameter, $e_{i,j}$, equal to that ratio. In addition, for any good I that is not produced by country J in the given scale economies equilibrium, the linear parameter is given a value so small that country J is not competitive in the production of good I. This procedure can always be carried out, subject only to the requirement that none of the calculated average productivity values for the scale economies model exceeds the maximal productivity figure for the same country and commodity in the linear model. This last requirement is the first of the two correspondence theorem preconditions that was mentioned in an earlier section.

Next suppose that we start with a family of linear models and plot the $2^n - 2$ of its maximal productivity equilibrium points that are perfectly specialized. Is there a scale economies model that yields exactly those same equilibrium points? In addition, if such a scale economies model exists, how can that model be determined? That is, given any such set of equilibria for a family of linear models, can we describe the scale economies model, if any exists, that yields the same equilibria? In answer, we can prove:

CORRESPONDENCE THEOREM 2   Any set of $2^n - 2$ equilibria, with different assignments of the traded goods for specialized production by the two countries and deriving from a family of linear models, will correspond to the equilibria of a single economies of scale model with n traded goods if and only if, for any two linear models in the family in question, the corresponding equilibria satisfy the following scale-economies–compatibility condition: If the equilibrium of one of two linear models in the given family lies to the right of the other, then the productivity level for any good I produced by country 1 at the rightward equilibrium point must be no higher than the corresponding productivity at the leftward equilibrium point. Similarly the productivity level for any good I' produced by country 2 must be no lower at the rightward equilibrium point than at the equilibrium point to its left.

The intuitive reasons underlying the theorem and its precondition are the following: In a scale economies model the productivity of labor must, by definition, rise as the amount of labor devoted to an industry increases. Now, as we move to the right in the graph, country 1's share of world income and of the world's industries increases. With a fixed labor force and full employment, this means that there must be a fall in employment in the average industry of the rising number of industries possessed by that country. Indeed, it is easy to prove that in our model employment in each of those industries must fall. Hence, if this move is to be consistent with scale economies, productivity in such an industry must decrease. Similarly, with a move to the right in the graph, country 2 must spread its fixed labor force over a smaller number of industries than before, increasing the quantity of labor per industry so that, if there are economies of scale, average labor productivity in country 2 must rise. Consequently only if the scale economies–compatibility condition of theorem 2 is satisfied by the family of linear models is it possible for there to exist a single scale economies model that can yield the same set of equilibria.

What is more, once the condition of the theorem is satisfied, it is not difficult to construct a single scale economies model that does the trick—that yields the selected $2^n - 2$ equilibria of the given family of linear models. For this purpose we recall that aside from the production functions, all the relationships and parameter values in a family of linear models are, by definition, identical. One then constructs the desired scale economies model in the following two steps: First, for all parts of the scale economies model other than its production function, use the relationships and parameter values common to the given family of linear models. Second, to complete the scale economies model, determine only its production function, call it $f_{i,j}(l_{i,j})$. To do this, at any of the selected equilibrium points, set the average product of labor of country J in good I, $f_{i,j}(l_{i,j})/l_{i,j}$, equal to the corresponding and fixed average productivity figure, $e_{i,j}$, in the linear model that yields the equilibrium in question. It should then be plausible that the resulting production relationship is what we are looking for. It has scale economies because it satisfies the scale economies–compatibility condition of the correspondence theorem 2, and it clearly shares all other pertinent relationships and parameter values with the given family of linear models.

The importance of that result for our purposes is that the unfamiliar features that have emerged from the growing literature on scale economies in international trade analysis are not peculiar to the scale economies case alone. Rather, these features arise also in the more familiar linear case whose well-known attributes may facilitate understanding of the new scale economies observations.

8.5 The Attributes of a Trading Partner Who Serves Country 1's Interests Ideally

Even if both countries gain by trading, the magnitude of the benefit to either of the parties depends on the number and identity of the industries that devolve upon the other, and the productive techniques its trading partner employs in those industries. The question we consider next is: What assignment of industries to country 2 and what levels of productivity of country 2 in the industries assigned to it will maximize the benefits of trade to country 1? That is, we will examine what assignment of outputs and what levels of productivity for country 2 will make it into the ideal trading partner for country 1, as evaluated exclusively in terms of country 1's selfish interests.

Let us first consider the case in which country 1 has attained maximal productivity in all of its industries. In terms of our graphs, the ideal trading partner for country 1 entails production arrangements for country 2 that bring country 1 as close as possible to the summit point on its absolute income (upper utility) frontier. Country 2's position, then, is shown by the dot marked A_1 in figure 8.1. Several things become apparent from this graph. First, because the peak of the country 1 frontier always lies to the right of that for country 2, we may expect that the ideal trading partner for country 1 will be one that produces a fairly limited share of the world's commodities. In the particular model resembling that in figure 8.1 (which entails 22 industries), only six of those products are supplied by country 2 when it is an ideal trading partner, with the remaining 16 produced by country 1. This result is not what standard analysis might have led us to expect. In this case, even in a world of evolving linear relationships (i.e., changing values of the productivity parameters), a country's welfare is enhanced by a very uneven distribution of industries among countries, with countries other than itself engaged in production of a very limited set of the world's traded commodities. Our result is more compatible with views common among nonspecialists, asserting simply that the ideal trading partner for country 1 is an economy that has succeeded in capturing a very modest share of the world's industries.

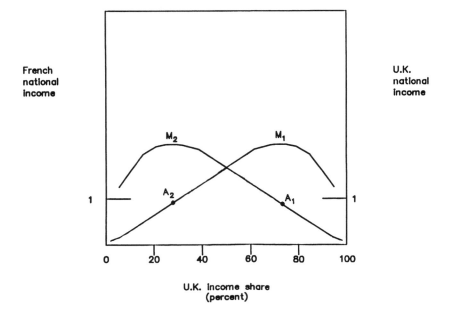

Figure 8.1
Ideal trading partners

The qualitative result is supported quantitatively by analysis of the special case where the maximal productivity levels are the same for both countries. In that situation it is possible to carry out rigorous calculations of general validity. Such a calculation shows that where the countries are identical in size (i.e., in the magnitude of their labor forces), a country's ideal trading partner will always turn out just 24 percent of the world's commodities.

The fact that the peak of country 1's upper income frontier lies to the right of that of country 2 also means that the position of ideal trading partner for country 1 entails a sacrifice for country 2 that can be substantial. When it is the ideal trading partner for country 1, country 2's equilibrium point (point A_1 in figure 8.1) lies well to the right of the peak, M_2, of its own upper income frontier. Thus country 2's ideal trading partner equilibrium point will lie below (and, plausibly, far below) the highest point in its own equilibrium region. Country 2 must give up some, and possibly a good deal, of its maximum potential income in order to qualify as an ideal trading partner for country 1.

A third observation emerges from the analysis of the preceding section. As is plausible intuitively, when a country is the sole producer of some good, a *ceteris paribus* increase in its productivity in that commodity will always benefit itself and the country with which it trades. Consequently, to serve as ideal trading partner, country 2 must always attain maximal productivity in each of the (few) industries in which it is a producer. This is again plausible. If Japan imports all of its oil, it obviously serves the interests of Japan if the petroleum-supplying nations produce oil as efficiently and cheaply as possible.

Finally, we see that the story can be very different when there is a rise in country 2's productivity in a commodity it is not initially producing. A substantial rise in such a productivity figure in, say, industry I can constitute a threat to country 1's position in that industry. It may enable country 2 to compete away some or all of the product I sales of country 1, thereby cutting the latter's real income. Thus the analysis sheds light on the effects upon the well-being in one country of an improvement in the productivity of its trading partner. The issue, for example, is whether the rise in productivity in a number of Japanese industries threatens the welfare of western Europe and the United States. More careful economic analysis has suggested that the matter is not open and shut. Viewed superficially, the standard theory seems to claim that a rise in productivity in one country must be beneficial to all. On this view, indeed, the benefits of increased world output and lower prices are generally transmitted throughout the globe, with trade barriers serving as a primary impediment to universal distribution of the gains. Our analysis does show that if country 1's trading partner initially produces an extremely small number of commodities, then a rise in the trading partner's productivity in at least a few of the industries from which it is initially excluded can be mutually beneficial. However, once the trading partner's share of the world's industries exceeds the modest number that makes it the ideal trading partner for country 1, then a further rise in country 2's productivity in commodities it is not initially producing threatens to cut the real income of country 1.

The possibility that country 1 can suffer a loss in welfare as a result of a rise in productivity in country 2 may, perhaps, be surprising at first, given the rise in total world output that is likely to result. But a simple observation may make the result more plausible. Consider a linear model with two countries of equal size and identical demand functions. If some but not all of the productivity parameters in country 1 are twice as high as those in country 2, with the other parameters equal in the two countries, then country 1 can expect to gain from trade and be better off than it would be in autarky. But if country 2 increases its productivity to the point where its productivity parameters are all equal in value to those of country 1, then all gains from trade will obviously disappear. Country 1 will be driven from a result that is better for itself than autarky to one that is no better than autarky, and it will have been the increase in country 2's productivity that is responsible for country 1's loss in welfare. To summarize, for a country to constitute an ideal trading partner, it must exhibit three characteristics. It must be the producer of a modest share of the traded commodities, leaving it with low relative wages and a small share of world income; it must be a maximally efficient producer of just those goods that it does supply; and it must be an inefficient producer of all the remaining commodities, so that it constitutes no competitive threat in those industries.

One can think of a number of low-income agricultural countries that are probably nearly ideal trading partners for some of the leading industrialized economies. We can also determine an upper bound for the relative level of wages in the country that is the ideal partner, at least in the case where the sizes of the labor forces and the maximal productivities in the two countries are the same. Where these conditions are satisfied, we can make use of the explicit general equation for the upper income frontier that this case permits, and show that the ratio of wages in the two countries can never fall far below 3:1. That is, the ideal trading partner is always condemned to have a real wage level that is, in circumstances most favorable to it, only slightly more than one-third as high as that in the other country. Clearly, from the point of view of the ideal trading partner, that status is far from ideal.

One further important conclusion follows from the analysis. A deviation of any sort in the country 2 parameter values from those of the ideal trading partner must be harmful to the interests of country 1. If the changed parameter values increase the real income of country 2, that must harm country 1. Similarly, if those parameter values change in a manner that reduces the real income of country 2, that must also harm country 1.

8.6 Evolving Productivity and Intertemporal Performance Patterns

The notion of a family of linear models can be used to explore growth in productivity and its consequences. For this purpose we need only compare a sequence of linear models, each with higher values of its productivity parameters than those of the model that preceded it in the sequence. We can then prove the intuitively plausible

THEOREM 3 (Convergence toward maximal productivity) In a model of learning-by-doing, technology transfer and the absence of erosion (obsolescence) of the stock of knowledge, all trajectories of the productivity levels of industries in which country J is a producer will converge toward that country's maximal productivity levels. That is, all trajectories will entail movement toward points within the region of maximal productivity.

This evolutionary path of a country's productivity returns us to an issue we dealt with in the previous section: the benefits and costs to a country as the productivity of its trading partner increases. We have already seen that this process will sometimes be advantageous and sometimes be disadvantageous to the country other than the one whose productivity levels are increasing. Frank Stafford of the University of Michigan (along with several coauthors) has, however, analyzed the subject in a different way, looking more closely at the consequences for the individual industries involved. It is useful to recapitulate briefly some of the most pertinent of the results of his investigation.

To facilitate the discussion, we will say that country 1 is uncompetitive in the production of good I if country 1 cannot supply I as cheaply as country 2. We will use the phrases, "Country 1 is competitive in good I" and "Both countries are marginally competitive in I," analogously. The results are most easily summarized by dividing the pertinent range of the changing productivity parameter into three zones: zone 1 in which country 2 is uncompetitive in I, zone 2 in which the two countries are marginally competitive in I, and zone 3 in which country 1 is uncompetitive in I. Then the analysis asserts that, so long as the two countries remain in zone 1, a rise in Country 2's I competitiveness has no effect on the income of either country. In zone 3, where country 2 is the sole producer of I, a rise in country 2's I productivity benefits both countries proportionately. However, in the central zone 2, where the two countries are and remain marginally competitive, a rise in country 2's I productivity benefits country 2 at country 1's expense. The higher the country 2 productivity level in that zone, the greater is the real income of country 2 and the smaller is the real income of country 1. It follows that country 2 is always unharmed and generally gains on balance from a rise in the average productivity of labor in some industry, and while in some circumstances the result can also be beneficial to country 1, in other circumstances the effect on country 1's real income will be unambiguously detrimental. Sophisticated trade theorists such as Jacob Viner would undoubtedly not have been shocked at this result that offers some legitimate grounds for the fears of nonspecialists about international trade rivalry, but the result does diverge from the conclusions suggested by some more naive discussions of trade theory.

Why does the theorem hold? The explanation is slightly different for the cases of the three zones, with that for the intermediate zone of universal marginal competitiveness perhaps the most difficult. The argument underlying the result for zone 1, in contrast, is trivial. In that zone, country 2 starts off and remains a non-producer of I because it is uncompetitive in that good. Consequently a rise in its competitiveness in that item has no effect on anything, because of the continued absence of any activity in that industry by country 2. At the other extreme, in zone 3, country 2 is the only producer of I. The growth in output per worker-hour in country 2 then makes the good steadily cheaper for both countries and so gives them both more of the good for a given expenditure. Something similar holds for country 2 in the intermediate zone 2, where both countries produce good I.

But why does country 1 lose out in zone 2 when country 2's productivity in good I rises? The answer, which was provided by the current authors (1995a), is not that country 1 receives less of good I. On the contrary, since country 1 produces some or all of the good I that it consumes, with the good I productivity of labor in that country constant, an hour of labor will earn just enough to purchase exactly as much of good I as before, despite the growth in the other country's I productivity. Curiously, country 1 loses out to a degree because it gets less to consume of some goods other than I. There are two cases in which this is clearly true. First, is the case of goods other than I of which country 2 continues to be the sole producer despite its rising productivity in good I. For, with the resulting increase in country 2 wages, imports of those items by country 1 will grow ever more expensive. The rising price does not damage the welfare of country 2 because its increased wage provides additional purchasing power that offsets the price rise. Country 1, however, obtains no such rising wage offset, so the increased prices of the goods it buys from country 2 reduce the real national income of country 1 but not that of country 2. The second case deals with goods that are transferred to country 2 from country 1 because rising wages in country 1 have made it uncompetitive in those commodities. Paradoxically, country 1 also loses out in getting less to consume of these goods in which it has become competitive. The reason is not far to seek. Consider a good I^*, which formerly was produced exclusively by country 2 at a price of $5. Suppose that country 1 could have produced that item for $6 per unit. Rising wages in country 2 resulting from increased I productivity now raise the cost of production of I^* in that country to $6.25, so country 2 becomes uncompetitive in production of good I^*. The cost to country 1 of a unit of good I^* therefore rises from our illustrative $5 to $6, without any offsetting rise in country 1 wages like that enjoyed by country 2. In the case of country 2, the wage offset is even more effective than it would have been if it had continued to be the producer of good I^* because the transfer of I^* production to country 1 limits the price rise to $6, rather than letting it go all the way to $6.25, as it would have to if country 2 were to have continued as I^* producer.

In sum, we see how rising I productivity in country 2 benefits it both by a greater abundance of good I, and by a rise in wages that at least keeps pace with the resulting rise in prices of other goods. But country 1 in this case loses out because rising country 2 prices increase the cost of country 1's imports, with no offsetting rise in country 1's purchasing power, despite any industries that may as a consequence be transferred to it from country 2.

The results must nevertheless be interpreted with caution. First, the discussion, as reported, takes no account of the premise of the analysis that at any time there is a ceiling upon each productivity parameter. Second, the increase in I productivity in country 2 may span several zones. It may, for instance, bring country 1 from being marginally competitive in good I (zone 2) to a state of uncompetitiveness in I (zone 3). Then country 1 will lose out from the rise in country 2's productivity when they were in zone 2, but the further rise in country 2's I productivity when zone 3 is attained will benefit country 1. The net gain or loss to country 1 from the entire change therefore cannot be determined in general terms by the analysis of this section. Only our basic graph, as employed in the preceding section, offers an unambiguous and general evaluation of the effects on a country's welfare of a rise in the productivity (and hence in the share of world income) of its trading partner.

9

Three-Country Models and Other Complications

Like any simplified theoretical construct, the model we have described so far has some features very different from what is observed in reality. However, if a model is useful, such features can be changed and adapted without undermining the important conclusions of the original, simpler version. We will take up that task in this chapter.

The most obvious example to discuss in our story is the premise that the world is composed of only two countries. Second, there is our discussion's assumed tendency of stable equilibria to be perfectly specialized, with no commodity produced in more than one country. Third, there is the obviously unrealistic situation toward both the rightward and leftward ends of our graph, where one country or the other finds itself driven from almost all of the world's industries. None of these phenomena are common in the real world. Few, if any, widely used products come from only a single country. This is true even of products with substantial scale economies. Moreover all countries produce many goods and services, even the countries with the very lowest per-capita incomes.

Our model can be modified to eliminate these three urealistic features. We will show explicitly how the three-country case can be dealt with, and by implication, how one can analyze trade among more than three countries. Both other anomalies are ascribable to two other unrealistic features of the model as described so far. These features, adopted for expository and analytic simplicity, are easily modified and with that modification the peculiarities described in the preceding paragraph also disappear. Both oversimplified premises relate to scale economies.

First, we have so far assumed that each and every one of the world's outputs is produced under conditions of economies of scale. Second, we have assumed that scale economies are never exhausted, no matter how large the volume of production of a good. That is, we have assumed that the larger the output of any item the cheaper it will always become, with no possibility that the size of an industry can become excessive from the viewpoint of productive efficiency. Both premises clearly require modification. Many goods are produced under conditions of diminishing returns, at least beyond some relatively modest level of output. And, as we will see, in our analysis there is no reason for countries, even those that are least developed, to be driven out of such industries when their relative incomes decline further, that is, as one approaches the vertical axis in the graph at which that country's share of world income is zero. Second, in many if not all of the industries in which scale economies are substantial, there comes a point where further expansion yields no additional efficiency benefits, so beyond that point total cost either rises proportionately when output expands, or rises even more rapidly than that. The implication is that equilibria tend to be characterized by a relatively small number of suppliers of any commodity, but not generally by just a single supplier.

We will proceed to deal with several other features of reality: nontraded goods, and a world containing both linear production and retainable industries. It turns out that none of these complications fundamentally affects our main results.

9.1   Graphs of Three-Country Models

As is true of much of the international trade literature, our analysis so far has been conducted with the aid of a two-country model. But as is well-known, results obtained for models containing only two countries or two goods or two critical entities of some other sort are not always valid when the number of such entities is increased to three or more (e.g., see Dixit and Norman 1980, p. 8, for just one of a number of examples provided in that book). In this chapter we will, however, demonstrate graphically that our main qualitative results continue to hold, albeit with some illuminating modifications, in a three-country world. The argument suggests also that the analysis remains fundamentally valid when more than three trading countries are contained in the analysis.

Figure 9.1 is the three dimensional representation of the world upper income boundary and the country 1 upper income boundary for the three-country case. These are the pertinent surfaces analogous to the

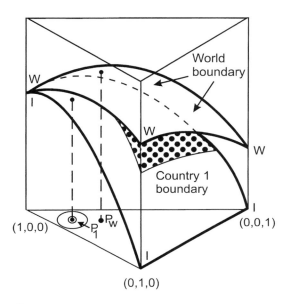

Figure 9.1
The three-country case I

world and country 1 boundaries in the two-country model. There are now three origins, at each of which two of the countries have zero share, while the share of the remaining country, J, is $Z_j = 1$, and three axes, one for each pair of countries, along which the share of the remaining country is zero. Thus the corner of the graph in the foreground is labeled (0, 1, 0), meaning that at this point countries 1 and 3 each have zero share of world income, while country 2 has 100 percent of that income. The axis to the right of that point ends at (0, 0, 1) where country 1 still has zero share, indicating that this is the $Z_1 = 0$ axis. The floor of the diagram constitutes an equilateral triangle, and any point inside it represents a division of world income among the three countries, with the coordinates of that point indicating the shares of the three countries, share of country J being indicated by the length of the line segment from the point in question to the $Z_j = 0$ axis, that line segment being drawn perpendicular to that axis.

The vertical axis represents absolute income, and the world upper income boundary is the hill-shaped surface, WWW. The country 1 surface is shown below the world boundary, and is obtained from the latter as before, from the expression $Y_1 = Z_1 Y_w$, where Y_w and Y_1 are, respectively, the absolute world income and country 1 income at any

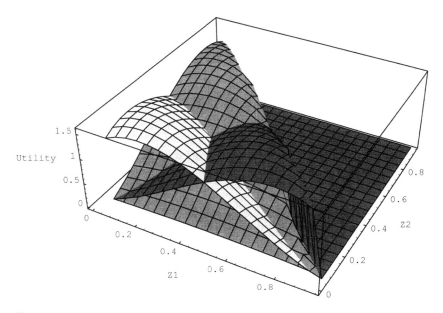

Figure 9.2
The three-country case II

given shares. That is, they are the heights of the two surfaces above any
selected point P on the floor of the graph. In particular, P_w, and P_1 correspond respectively to the peaks of the two surfaces. As before, P_1
must lie closer to point $(1, 0, 0)$ than does P_w if the surfaces are differ-
entiable and concave, because at P_w (where the partial derivative of Y_w
with respect to the share of any country must be zero) we must have,
differentiating with respect to Z_1, $Y_1' = Z_1Y_w' + Y_w = Y_w > 0$.

Figure 9.2 is a computer-generated graph for a particular illustrative
model, showing the upper boundaries for all three countries.

9.2 Zones of Pure Conflict, Pure Mutual Gain and
Multiple Possibilities

Figure 9.3 is the projection for all three countries on the base of figure
9.1. In the three-country case, as we have seen, the horizontal projection of the relevant graph is an equilateral triangle with the length of
each side equal to unity. It corresponds to the horizontal axis in the
two-country graph. The points P_1, P_2, and P_3 are the projections of the

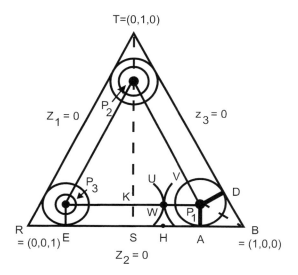

Figure 9.3
Projection: Three-country equilibria

income peaks of the three countries and the curves surrounding those
points are iso-national income (contour) curves. For simplicity of discussion, we assume perfect symmetry, with the peak for each of the
three countries located in exactly the same position relative to its adjacent origin (the points R, B, and T). The iso-income curves surrounding the three peaks are drawn, also for simplicity, to be circular.

As far as regions of conflict and mutual gain are concerned, we will
see that matters are now rather more complicated than in the two-
country model. Because there are regions in which moves can either
benefit or harm some or all of the countries, we speak of three kinds
of region: the zone of pure conflict, the zone of pure mutual gain and
the zone of multiple possibilities. In the sequel, for brevity the term
"pure" will be omitted when discussing the zone of conflict and the
zone of mutual gain, with the adjective, however, always to be kept in
mind. We will show that the zone of conflict in figure 9.3 is the interior
of the smaller triangle joining the three country peaks. Specifically, it
will be seen that:

PROPOSITION 1   Some country always loses from a move in the
zone of conflict. Starting from any point in the interior of this triangle,

any move to another such point must harm at least one of the countries.

This result is obvious, for any such step must move the equilibrium point further from one of the corners of the inner triangle. Hence this situation must yield a reduced income to the country whose income peak is located at that corner.

The zone of conflict for any pair of countries taken by themselves is a portion of the corresponding axis. For example, for trade between countries 1 and 3, with country 2 totally excluded from trade, the zone of conflict is the portion of the horizontal axis, EA, directly below the inner triangle. If we use r as the length of EA, since the length of the horizontal axis is $RB = 1$, the share of the zone of conflict in a two-country model becomes $EA/RB = r$. The corresponding figure for the three-country case is the ratio of the areas of the two triangles, area $P_1P_2P_3$/area $RBT = r^2$. Hence, since $r < 1$, it follows that in the three-country case the zone of pure conflict becomes relatively smaller than it is in the two-country case.

While in the two-country case we had only zones of conflict and zones of mutual gain, we now have a much greater and more varied list of possibilities. Furthermore the interpretation of the remaining zones becomes more complex in the three-country case. There, starting from any point, there will generally exist moves that benefit all three countries, but it is also possible to move in directions that are damaging to any one, or any pair or even all three of the countries. A mutually beneficial move from such a point may also require one country to give up industries to both of the others (in regions such as $ABDP_1$) or two of the countries to give up industries to the third, as in region EAP_1P_3. We turn now to explanation of these assertions. We will interpret the three quadrilateral regions such as $ABDP_1$, which include a corner of the large triangle, as the zones of mutual gain. In contrast, the three rectangular regions, such as EAP_1P_3, will be considered zones of multiple possibilities, a concept that is explained in the next section.

9.3   Interpretation and Sizes of the Subregions

The area of the entire triangle RBT is determined by its two attributes: that it is an equilateral triangle, with sides of length unity. (Its area is half the product of ST and RB, a product which equals 0.5 length ST, since $RB = 1$. But $ST = (BT^2 - SB^2)^{1/2} = (1 - 0.25)^{1/2} = 0.89$ approximately. So the area of that entire triangle is approximately half that amount, 0.445. But this number does not really matter for our analysis.) The smaller inner triangle is also equilateral, with each side of length r, so that the vertical line segment, KP_2 has length rST, and therefore the area of the inner triangle clearly is r^2 times the area of the larger triangle.[1] This demonstrates, since $r^2 < r$, that the zone of conflict is a smaller share of the total region in the case of three countries than it is when only two countries are included in the model.

Next, we show that the remaining zones are as was just described. We have assumed that the iso-income curves of country 1 are circles with the peak of country 1 at the center. Then the zone of mutual gain generated by that peak includes the quadrilateral region $ABDP_1$, as well as the two corresponding quadrilateral regions corresponding to the peaks of the other two countries. These are interpretable as zones of mutual gain because everywhere in the region $ABDP_1$, for example (in analogy with the zone of mutual gain in the two-country case), the incomes of all three countries will be declining as country 1 moves from its peak toward large triangle corner B, thereby increasing its share, Z_1, toward unity. Looked at in the opposite way, in this region, starting from a point near triangle corner B, country 1 always gains by moving upward and to the left, taking the shortest path toward its peak, P_1, thereby increasing the shares of both other countries and benefiting them both as well as itself.

In the rectangle EAP_1P_3 matters are different. Since the iso-income curves of any one country are concentric circles, the line segment P_3P_1 is the locus of points of tangency between the iso-income curves of countries 1 and 3. Consequently any point below that line segment will be surrounded by two such tangent curves. For example, point H is surrounded by the two curves U (for country 3) and V (for country 1), that are tangent at W. This means that a move from H to W must benefit all three countries. But such a move gives country 2 more industries at the expense of both other countries. In other words, such a mutually beneficial move can require the coordination of policy of developed countries 1 and 3 to get them both to agree to give up industries to underdeveloped country 2.

More important, examination of the graph readily confirms that starting from a point above H in the rectangular region there are moves that are damaging to any one preselected country, moves that harm any pair of the three countries, and moves (straight downward) that are detrimental to all three. We therefore refer to the three rectangular areas like EAP_1P_3 as zones of multiple possibilities.

To find the size of region $ABDP_1$, one of the three zones of mutual gain, note that it is made up of two identical 30–60–90 degree triangles, ABP_1 and DBP_1. This is so since A and D are right angles and B is a 60 degree angle. For comparability with the two-country case, we take $AB = 0.5(1 - r) = DB$. Write $s = 0.5(1 - r)$. For a two-country model, the share of the zone of mutual gain is $1 - r = 1s$. For the three-country model, note first that, with DBP_1 a 30 degree angle, its tangent is 0.58. Thus we have $DP_1 = 0.58s$, so the area of this subzone of mutual gain is twice that of triangle DBP_1, or $0.58s^2$. The total area of the three corner zones of mutual gain, one adjacent to each country peak, is approximately $1.73s^2$, and its share of the area of the total triangle RBT is $s^2(1.73/0.445) = 3.9s^2$, approximately. Since $s \leq 0.5$, because $2s$, the size of the two-country zone of mutual gain, cannot exceed unity (and s is likely to be far less than 0.5), we have $s^2 (3.9) < 2s$; that is, the corner zones of mutual gain in the three-country case must add up to a smaller (and presumably far smaller) share of the region of equilibria in the three-country case than in the case of two countries.

We also note that since $\tan 30° = 0.58$, then P_1B must be almost twice as long as $P_1D = AP_1$. But the move from P_1 to D amounts to reduction of the share of country 3 to zero, while the move from P_1 to A reduces country 2's share to zero. In contrast, a move from P_1 to B entails reduction to zero of the shares of *both* country 2 and country 3. This implies that the latter (two-country deprivation) move will entail a larger loss of income to country 1 (a move to a lower iso-income curve) than will either of the former (one-country deprivation) moves.

This completes our discussion of the three-country model.

9.4   A Mixture of Retainable and Linear-Production Industries

In chapter 3 we populated our model of the trading world exclusively with retainable industries. In chapter 4 we examined industries that were not retainable but whose production was linear and whose productivity could be changed, by acquisition of the skills required to raise productivity. Each of these chapters, following the dictates of simplicity, described an unmixed model. In the one case, all the industries were assumed to be retainable, while in the other case, all the industries were linear with a wide range of possible productivity levels. Here we will mix the two, as is true in reality, where some industries are retainable and some are not.

It will not be surprising that the composite model behaves very similarly to the simpler unmixed versions, since our results in the two cases were so similar. If some of the industries entering into international trade are retainable, and the others face a range of productivity levels, we obtain substantially the same diagrams as before. There are variations, but these variations do not affect the economic conclusions.

More specifically, what we find is that the upper boundary of the region of equilibria still has its characteristic shape, a hill-shaped region with a single hilltop. The difference, it can be shown, is that there is a lower boundary over part of the diagram, and the region is filled in solidly to the bottom of the graph in part of the diagram. While the resulting boundaries are different from those of the simpler models, they are not different in the part of the diagram that matters for our economic conclusions. The upper boundary is the same, though the lower boundary is different. But it is those upper boundary shapes that determine the conflicts between the best outcomes for the two trading partners. The U.K. hilltop outcome is still bad for France and the French hilltop is still bad for the U.K. The new lower boundary does not affect the outcome.

9.5   Goods with Fixed Productivity Coefficients Subject to Diminishing Returns

There are two clear reasons why even countries that are impoverished and earn a minuscule proportion of the world's GDP nevertheless produce a substantial variety of products, contrary to the implication of the most simplified variant of our model. First, there are many items, notably personal services, that do not enter international trade at all, or of which a considerable portion is produced only for domestic use. The overused illustration is haircuts. These nontraded goods are treated in section 9.12.

Besides ignoring nontraded goods, our model has up to now dealt in a special way with goods whose production process is characterized by diminishing or even constant returns to scale. Up to now, we have studied how the equilibrium in a world of such goods changes as productivity grows. Now we will briefly examine what occurs in our analysis when such goods, like the goods with scale economies, have productivity values that do not change during the period studied, and the economy contains both types of goods—scale economies and scale diseconomies products. Since the real world does contain both, it is clearly desirable to incorporate such diminishing-returns goods and services into the model, and it is not too difficult to do. But before we explain how we do it and describe the implications of this modification in our model, we must review briefly several important and very well-known features of the diminishing-returns case.

Many Small and Competing Producers

A diminishing-returns industry is characterized by the presence of a substantial number of small producers in direct competition with one another. Since, in such an industry, small is economical and large is expensive, competitive market forces will prevent any firm from growing very large. For similar reasons its products are generally produced simultaneously in many countries. Which economy, for example, is entirely without an agricultural sector?

Asymmetry in the Competition between Industrialized Economies and LDCs (Less-Developed Countries)

All asymmetry means is that with diminishing returns, even if all the industries with substantial scale economies are taken over by the dozen or so advanced industrial countries, the other countries will still be able to participate in the remaining industries, with scale diseconomies or constant returns to scale. However, the less-developed countries do not generally find themselves alone in such activities. Industrialized countries are not necessarily more handicapped as suppliers of diminishing-returns products than any other nations, so long as their superior technology offsets the higher wages of the wealthier countries. The United States continues to be one of the world's leading agricultural producers, in competition with many of the less-developed countries. In other words, while the United States faces no competition from less-developed economies in the manufacture of large passenger aircraft, the LDC's continue to encounter the American farmer as a rival in the grain market.

Equal Marginal–Cost Ratios

A last, well-known implication of diminishing returns is critical for their incorporation into our analysis. Elementary economic theory tells us that in competitive markets if two goods, call them A and B, are supplied simultaneously by two producers, X and Y, then in equilibrium the ratio of the marginal costs of the two products to supplier X must be equal to the corresponding ratio for supplier Y, and both of these must be equal to the ratio of the market prices of the two goods. Indeed, where any one producer is sufficiently small to be deprived of any influence over world price, which is clearly to be expected in a diminishing-returns scenario, it must be true that in a stable equilibrium any commodity that is produced simultaneously in two countries must have the same marginal cost in both countries, and that common marginal cost must be equal to the international price of that item (expressing the currencies of the two counties in common terms, say, in dollars at the current exchange rate).

9.6 Inclusion of Products with Diminishing Returns to Scale: Hints on Method and Results

We have also extended our analysis to the case where some industries operate under economies of scale while others are subject to diseconomies. Very roughly, in the calculation procedure one first separates out the scale economies and scale diseconomies industries. The scale economies industries are analyzed just as in chapters 2 and 3. However, the scale diseconomies industries, since they generally entail production by both countries, are constrained by the requirement that in equilibrium the marginal cost of any good supplied simultaneously by both countries must be the same in country 1 as in country 2. As an example, let us indicate how one can now go about finding the point on the country 1 upper frontier of the region of equilibria, corresponding to any given point on the horizontal axis of the graph. For this purpose, one solves the linear program that maximizes country 1's national income, subject to the normal requirements of equilibrium as the constraints of the program, as before, but adding to those constraints the requirement that the marginal costs of any diminishing-returns commodities produced in both countries be equal to one another.

The general results of this analysis[2] are illustrated in the four graphs of figure 9.4a–d, and contrast with figure 3.2, our basic graph on page 29 in chapter 3. The two ends of figure 3.2 depict the sort of extreme situations already reviewed at the beginning of this chapter. Near either vertical axis, one of the countries has been shut out of most trade activities, with the other nation having co-opted almost every product for

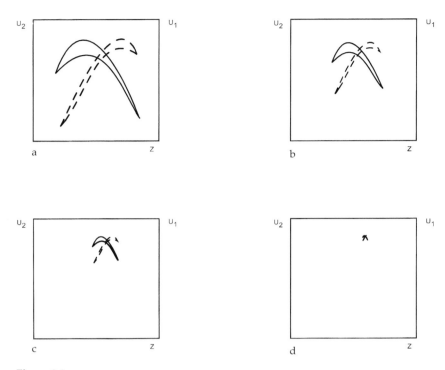

Figure 9.4
Shrinking region of equilibria when share of diminishing-returns industries grows

itself. In contrast, figure 9.4a–d shows a steady contraction from a large region of equilibria toward a single point. While in the basic graph all products are characterized by scale economies, in our new series of graphs the share of diminishing-returns products varies from 25 percent (in figure 9.4a) to 50, to 75 and, finally, to 95 percent of the total in the succeeding graphs. In all of these new graphs, even the last, the national income frontiers retain their characteristic hill shape, and in every figure in the central areas the gains of one country tend to come at the expense of the other. But as scale diseconomies dominate the world economy increasingly, the horizontal range over which the frontiers extend grows increasingly narrow, and the vertical range over which national income values extend also diminishes. Finally, when the world is exclusively devoted to the production of items with scale diseconomies, the frontiers of the two economies degenerate into a single and common point. This point corresponds to the single Ricardian equilibrium point in the classical model of international trade with its world of diminishing or constant returns, so that our analysis meshes perfectly with the classical analysis.

Why does this contraction of the region of equilibria happen? The answer is straightforward. One country can conceivably acquire for itself all or nearly all of the *scale economies* industries in the world, driving the other country out of these fields of activity. However, as we have seen, a country cannot in the same way drive another out of the production of a commodity that is subject to diminishing returns. The fact that even a poor nation can retain a position in production of these items places a floor under that poor nation's relative income—its relative income therefore can never be driven to zero. This prevents any equilibrium from occurring very near the left-hand end of the graph (where, in terms of the illustrative designations of the countries in earlier chapters, the relative income of the U.K. is close to zero) and does the same for points very close to the rightward end of the graph, where the relative income of France is near zero. This immediately forces a contraction of the region of equilibria away from the edges of the graph and toward its center. Moreover it should be evident why this contraction will be greater the smaller the proportion of scale-economies products among the world's outputs: When the share of such products is small, the share of industries from which any country can potentially be excluded is correspondingly reduced, and the larger its minimum relative income will consequently be. Clearly, a large minimum for the relative income of each country means that the region of equilibria must be far from either the rightward and the leftward ends of the graph.

The reason that the region shrinks toward a single point as diminishing-returns products near 100 percent of the world's outputs is also not difficult to envision. When all products are subject to diminishing returns, all countries can, prospectively, share in the production of every good. Thus competition is universal and unimpeded by startup costs, and the diminishing-returns attribute means that entry on a small scale into any industry provides a cost advantage rather than constituting a handicap. The result is that any production arrangement that is inefficient or does not most effectively serve the preferences of consumers cannot long endure. Such an arrangement will constitute a standing invitation for the entry of firms that can produce more efficiently or serve consumer preferences more effectively than the incumbent producers are doing. Thus, in a world of universal diminishing returns only one equilibrium will generally be possible. It is the equilibrium extolled by classical economics as the virtuous end-product of a regime of perfect competition—the equilibrium that maximizes the general welfare, given the distribution of income and the constraints constituted by limited availability of resources and the state of technological knowledge.

9.7   Extreme Cases: Many Producers or One Producer of a Given Commodity

We have now reviewed two polar scenarios in terms of the number of countries in which, according to the model, a particular commodity will be produced. At the one extreme, the case of ubiquitous scale diseconomies, the norm is production in many countries of any commodity for which world demand is substantial. The reasons have just been reviewed, and indeed, we encounter many examples of this sort in reality. The production of textiles, footwear, grains, and many other such items is widely diffused among the world's countries.

The other extreme case, the focus of earlier chapters, is considerably less realistic in this regard. For in the theoretical case of universal and substantial scale economies that continue whatever the volume of production of a good, single-country production is the rule. Any arrangement in which an item is produced in two such economies is inherently unstable. That is now easily seen with the aid of the proposition on the equality of marginal costs described earlier in this chapter. In any equilibrium in which a given commodity is produced in each of two countries, the marginal costs can be expected to be equal in the two countries. The argument for this conclusion continues to apply even under scale economies.[3] In such a situation, if either producer happens to expand its output even slightly, its marginal costs will be reduced below that of its rival. That competitive edge will enable the former to expand even further, each such move adding to its competitive advantage until, finally, the rival is driven from the field altogether.[4] That, in essence, is why in the theoretical case of universal scale economies unbounded in the range of outputs over which they prevail, we expect not only that some stable equilibria will be perfectly specialized, but that stability requires all candidate equilibria to be so.

The assumption of persistence of scale economies that is critical here is that scale economies must result from any expansion of output of good I whether the initial volume of output of I happens to be relatively small, intermediate, or very great. Whether a supplier of I happens to be producing ten or ten thousand or ten million units of its output per year, it is critical to assume for perfect specialization to occur that any further expansion in the amount it is producing, whether minuscule or very large, will reduce its marginal and/or its average cost. There must come no point in the relevant range of output at which it will have used up all the available opportunities for further scale economies.

9.8   Bounded Scale Economies and Multiple Producers of a Good

The empirical evidence and casual observation suggest that reality is not like that. Few, if any, goods with any substantial demand are supplied by only a single country, and few, if any, goods benefit from scale economies that are not exhausted beyond some volume of production. The empirical evidence, it is true, indicates that scale economies are hardly rare (e.g., see Nadiri and Banani 1999, especially table 3, pp. 30–31). But the studies of particular industries that report the presence of scale economies at current output levels offer no reason to conclude that all further expansions of output will continue to yield additional economies.

Discussions with experienced businesspeople suggest that a pattern rather different from unbounded scale economies is far more common. They have come to expect, on the basis of their experience, that there will indeed be substantial savings that expansion of output can initially provide. Beyond some point, however, costs will tend to increase more or less proportionately when output expands further. This view often leads business statisticians who seek to estimate the firm's cost function to specify a relationship consistent with sharp initial scale economies followed by a linear segment along which marginal costs are constant.

The empirical evidence seems to be consistent with the hypothesis that a cost pattern something like that is common. A number of studies report evidence of this phenomenon. In the literature it is commonly referred to as the "flat-bottomed average cost curve." This is an average-cost curve (figure 9.5) in which average cost initially descends, perhaps rapidly, when volume rises. Ultimately, however, toward the right-hand end of the graph, average costs rise, as excessive size brings with it bureaucratization, communication problems, loss of personal

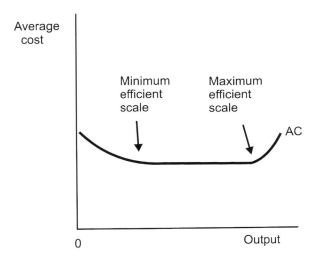

Figure 9.5
Flat-bottomed average-cost curve

touch, and the like. In between, in such a case, there is a (presumably considerable) output range in which average cost is horizontal, neither increased nor reduced by expansion. This is an activity whose scale economies are bounded.

Here the importance of flat-bottomed cost curves is that they characteristically result in equilibria with several producers supplying the commodity in question. Indeed, it is not only easy to see why this is so, but also to indicate the cost influences that may determine the number of producers of such a commodity. It should, however, be clear already that where the average cost curve is flat-bottomed the forces making for perfect specialization are undercut. So long as the quantity of the product demanded permits several suppliers to take full advantage of the available scale economies—that is, if each supplier can produce enough to end up in the flat-bottomed section of the curve— then none of them can gain any advantage over the others by further expansion. In short, so long as they all operate in the flat-bottomed portion of the curve, several suppliers of the commodity can coexist profitably. We can learn considerably more about the resulting multi-supplier equilibrium.

9.9   Efficient Number of Suppliers of a Commodity with a Flat-Bottomed Average-Cost Curve

We have already noted that competitive market forces can drive the economy toward efficient arrangements, though we have also seen that, where scale economies are present, candidate equilibria that are stable and yet inefficient are not only possible but can even be common. Yet it is useful to ignore this phenomenon for now and consider the number of suppliers required for efficiency in providing a commodity with a flat-bottomed average-cost (AC) curve.

That number depends on three things: the locations of the lower and upper ends of the range of horizontal average cost and the total amount of the commodity that is purchased in the world market. The lower end of the flat segment of the curve is referred to as a producer's minimum efficient scale. It is the smallest level of output at which the supplier's average cost is reduced to its lowest attainable level; that is, it is the output at which economies of scale are exhausted. Similarly one may refer to the largest output on the flat segment as the maximum efficient scale.

Now suppose that every supplier of a given commodity were to produce at its minimum efficient scale. Then total world output of that item would clearly equal minimum efficient scale multiplied by the number of producers. Thus, with supply equal to demand, we must have:

$$\text{Number of producers } (N_{min}) = \frac{\text{Total amount of the commodity purchased}}{\text{Minimum efficient scale}}$$

This intuitive result tells us that the greater the amount of the commodity demanded, the greater the number of producers it will require to meet that demand, given that each of them is producing at minimum efficient scale.

Exactly the same reasoning applies if the producers are each providing an output quantity equal to maximum efficient scale:

$$\text{Number of producers } (N_{max}) = \frac{\text{Total amount of commodity purchased}}{\text{Maximum efficient scale}}$$

The market will obviously provide room for fewer suppliers when they all operate at maximum efficient scale than when they each produce at minimum efficient scale, given the amount that is purchased. For if each supplier produces the larger quantity, it will require fewer suppliers to provide the total quantity that is purchased.

We conclude that the minimum number of suppliers that can produce the given world purchase quantity is obtained when each firm produces at maximum efficient scale, while the maximum efficient number of suppliers is that corresponding to the case where each supplier produces at minimum efficient scale. However, efficiency is also attained when some suppliers produce at minimum efficient scale, some at maximum efficient scale, and some produce an output that lies in between the two. Then efficiency will clearly be preserved because each supplier will still be operating somewhere along the flat and lowest segment of the AC curve, and the number of suppliers needed to meet world demand will be somewhere in between the two extreme cases that have just been described. That is, efficiency requires that the number of firms is given by any number between N_{min} and N_{max}.[5]

We can now readily see what is to be expected if market forces do drive the world economy toward an efficient equilibrium. In that case, if the number of nations supplying a commodity is below its maximum, then there is room for another nation to enter without displacement of any of the others. To succeed in its attempt, the entering country will have to produce at least at minimum efficient scale. The result of its successful entry will be some reduction in the sales of some or all of the incumbents, but it will not require any of them to be ejected. In contrast, if the number of suppliers is already at its maximum, then successful entry by a nation that was previously not providing the good will mean that some current supplier will find itself unable to retain its position in the field. Because its sales will be driven below minimum efficient scale, it will be unable to compete, having to charge a price above that prevailing in the market if it is to cover its costs.

9.10 General Characteristics of a Market with a Flat-Bottomed Average-Cost Curve

Several attributes of the case of the flat-bottomed average-cost curves can now readily be recognized. First, as already noted, unless demand for the commodity is very limited, it is characterized by simultaneous production of the commodity by several suppliers. Second, even here, a country that is initially not producing the commodity will find entry difficult, because success in that undertaking requires production on at least the minimum efficient scale virtually from the beginning. Third, entry into such an industry is indeed possible, and once entry has succeeded, the new supplier can feel a degree of confidence that displacement of its new position will not be easy. In other words, such an industry is retainable. Fourth, even if the number of suppliers of the good is initially less than the maximum, entry will come at the expense of the incumbents, who will find that they have lost sales as a result. In other words, entry is inherently an act of direct rivalry. Finally, the rivalrous character of the entry process takes its extreme and most obvious form when the number of suppliers is initially at its maximum, so that success of an entrant necessitates departure of an incumbent.

9.11   Divided Industries

The analysis of the retainable industries model in chapter 3 emphasized the perfectly specialized case that is simplest to analyze, that is, the case in which only one country is an active producer in any given industry. But we also asserted there that our results about conflict in international trade hold just as well when nonspecialized industries are included in the model, that is, when, despite high entry costs, industries are shared between countries. We now show why the inclusion of shared industries in our model does not affect the conclusions we reached earlier from the simpler specialized industries model.

To illustrate this point, we will compare graphs like those generated in chapter 3 with graphs to which shared industry outcomes have been added. For this purpose we have modeled a world of nine industries and two countries. Inclusion of all outcomes, not just those that are specialized, in the retainability model of chapter 3 has the effect illustrated in figure 9.6a and b. In figure 9.6a, we see the specialized equilibria for the U.K. generated by the nine-industry model. The more than 500 specialized outcomes are the black dots between the upper and lower boundaries. If in addition we now include all the nonspecialized equilibrium outcomes—that is, the equilibria in which there are industries that are shared between the two trading partners—we obtain a whole new array of equilibrium outcomes. These are the gray dots in figure 9.6b. These new shared-industry outcomes are much more numerous than the specialized ones. In this example, there are more than 18,000 nonspecialized outcomes. However, despite their great numbers, they do not substantially change the shape of the region of equilibria.

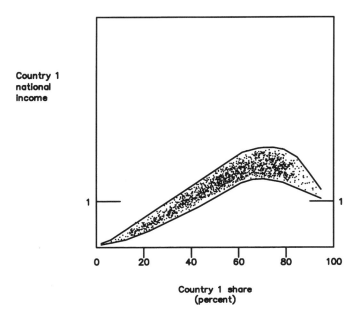

Figure 9.6a
Specialized equilibria

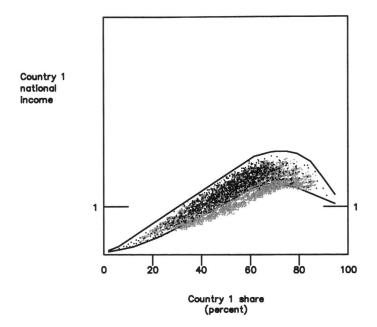

Figure 9.6b
Specialized and unspecialized equilibria

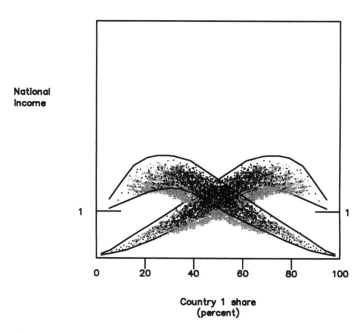

Figure 9.6c
The two countries with unspecialized equilibria

Figure 9.6b shows that most of the new shared-industry outcomes lie in and around the specialized ones. The main effect of including them is only to fill out more completely the region between the upper and lower boundary curves, but without changing its shape. The remaining shared-industry outcomes all lie below this region. None lies above it. For any given U.K. share, these low-lying equilibria represent outcomes that are worse than any specialized outcome with the same share. These outcomes are very poor because they contain many industries that are divided between the countries. Production tends to be costly in each of these divided industries because in each such industry no one country obtains the full cost-saving benefits of operation on the largest possible scale. Each such industry therefore produces in a more costly fashion than it would if the industry were concentrated in one country or the other. Many such divided industries can produce a very poor outcome.

In figure 9.6c we show all the outcomes for both countries. We can see from this figure, which is typical of the graphs obtained by including shared outcomes, that the presence of the shared industries does not change our conclusions about conflict in international trade. The graph for each country still retains its familiar hill shape, and the top of the hill for the U.K. is still a low point for France. The addition of all the equilibrium outcomes has not changed our fundamental conclusion: The outcomes that are best for one country still tend to be poor for the other.

9.12 Goods and Services Not Traded Internationally

Home construction and retailing are clear examples of goods and services that are rarely traded internationally. These goods and services are provided in each country mainly by those who work there. This category is enormous. It includes health care, transportation, the provision of local telephone service, haircutting, legal services, and so on, in an almost endless list of economic activities that are primarily domestic. An economy produces almost all of these goods and services at home and for home consumption, and this provides a large, relatively stable, base sector of national income consisting of goods and services that are exchanged almost entirely within its own borders.

Our analysis so far has dealt with the (internationally) traded sector only, the sector containing the industries that can be won or lost to international competition. We have discussed industries in which a country can have an entrenched position as a world supplier in a retainable industry. Or, in our linear production model, it can lose an industry position to another country whose productivity grows, or equally well, it can improve its own capabilities and acquire the world market in something another country used to make. None of this applies to haircutting or health care, nor to any of the other nontraded goods in the economy, so they have had no role in our analysis.

But it is not hard to add this sector to our model, and we have done so for the U.K. in figure 9.7. The graph has exactly the same shape as before, but the height of every equilibrium point has been raised by the addition of the dollar value of the goods produced in the nontraded sector of the U.K. In other words, in figure 9.7 the contribution to national income from the traded sector of the economy literally sits on top of that from the nontraded sector. We continue to use share of traded goods as our horizontal measure. But now, if the U.K. has lost out in every traded industry, and has zero share of international trade, it still can fall back on a substantial national income produced by all the things it makes and consumes at home. Our graph has exactly the

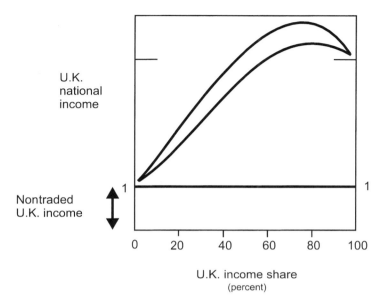

Figure 9.7
Equilibrium region with nontraded goods

same shape as before. The addition of the nontraded economy has simply raised every point in the graph.

Since the shape of the graph is unchanged by the inclusion of the nontraded sector, our conclusions about conflict in international trade are unchanged also. There is still conflict, and what is best for one country is still poor for the other one. With the international trade part of the graph now added to by the relatively unchanging base of domestic production, the outcomes that were originally undesirable for one of the countries are now not quite as bad, because the disadvantaged country's income is bolstered by the nontraded sector. Similarly the benefits to a country contributed by an equilibrium that serves its interests well are not quite as dramatically different from those of a less beneficial equilibrium, because the difference between the two equilibria now only represents an improvement over what may be a substantial base of internal economic activity.

Nevertheless, the effects of a change in outcome can still be very substantial. Exactly how large they are depends of the relative size of the traded and nontraded parts of the economy. The ups and downs of international trade cannot affect a country that, for one reason or another, barely participates in it. But there are few isolated countries left in the industrialized world, and there is a marked trend of growing internationalization of industries and growth in the traded sector, thus steadily increasing the relative magnitude of the effects we have described.

Two clear examples of this trend are the entertainment industry and the field of industrial design. In the past, a visit by a foreign theater company or an orchestra from another country was a rare, costly, and noteworthy event. Today television broadcasts and recordings cross oceans regularly with speed and ease. Similarly, for example, industrial blueprints were, until recently, typically created at sites that were in close physical proximity to those in which engineers worked. Today U.S. engineers can have blueprints prepared in India at lower cost and with no delay.

9.13   Conclusion

We have seen in this chapter that the analysis of this book is readily modified to incorporate various features of reality. We have extended the model to the multi-country case. Some new features do arise in that case, notably the zone of multiple possibilities. We have also seen that as the number of countries grows, the relative sizes of both the zone of conflict and the zone of mutual gain shrink in comparison to the total region of equilibria. But the fundamental point remains intact: There is conflict in the interests of countries similar in their wealth, while the wealthier countries can gain by improvements in the incomes of impecunious countries.

We have seen how the logic of our model can be modified to deal with the presence of a number of commodities characterized by diminishing returns to scale and how one can incorporate goods that benefit from scale economies up to some level of output, beyond which further gains from scale are exhausted. The former modification leads us to expect both a smaller region of equilibria and a considerable multiplicity of countries engaged in the production of overlapping sets of commodities. The latter modification also entails the likelihood of multi-country production of the commodities in question, though it is plausible that the number of producers of a given good with bounded scale economies will typically be smaller than that for a diminishing returns commodity. Finally, the case of bounded scale economies is characterized by a degree of direct rivalry among the nations supplying a given product that has no counterpart in the diminishing-returns cases. A nation initially excluded from production of that item may be able to embark successfully on its production but only at a sufficient initial scale of output. In addition it may well entail direct displacement of one of the nations initially participating in production of the item. This surely is what noneconomists have in mind when they express the fear that some industry in their economy will be unable to compete, with consequent loss of the industry to a foreign rival.

In this chapter we also stepped a little closer to the actual world by adding a few other elements of realism to our basic model. First, we examined models whose outcomes include equilibria in which some industries are not specialized. In other words, we dropped our simplifying assumption that each and every industry operates in only one producing country and looked at a more realistic world, where even for retainable industries, there are outcomes in which the production of some or all industries is divided between countries. Next, we dropped the premise that all goods and services in the world must be traded in the international marketplace, moving to a model that includes those many tangible and intangible products that never leave their home country. Finally, we looked briefly at situations where we neither assume, as we did in chapter 3, that all industries are retainable nor, as we did in chapter 4, that all are not retainable. We included in our analysis situations in which some industries have high start-up costs and economies of scale, and some do not. The basic overall conclusion is that none of these modifications of the model changes our results about inherent conflict in international trade or about the regions of mutual gain.

10   Predecessors

Nothing is more usual, among states which have made some advances in commerce, than to look on the progress of their neighbors with a suspicious eye, to consider all trading states as their rivals, and to suppose that it is impossible for them to flourish, but at their expense. In opposition to this narrow and malignant opinion, I will venture to assert, that the increase of riches and commerce in any one nation, instead of hurting, commonly promotes the riches and commerce of all its neighbors; and that a state can scarcely carry its trade and industry very far, where all the surrounding states are buried in ignorance, sloth, and barbarism. (David Hume, "Of the Jealousy of Trade," *Essays* (1741–42))

[Opponents of support of new industry by government offer] the proposition, that industry, if left to itself, will naturally find its way to the most useful and profitable employment. Whence it is inferred that manufactures, without the aid of government, will grow up as soon and as fast as the natural state of things and the interest of the community may require.

Against the solidity of this hypothesis . . . very cogent reasons may be offered. These have relation to the strong influence of habit and the spirit of imitation; the fear of want of success in untried enterprises; the intrinsic difficulties incident to first essays towards a competition with those who have previously attained to perfection in the business to be attempted: the bounties, premiums, and other artificial encouragements with which foreign nations second the exertions of their own citizens, in the branches in which they are to be rivaled. (Alexander Hamilton, *Report on Manufactures,* 1791, p. 203)

Much of what has been described in this book builds upon the fundamental contributions of earlier writers. This chapter is intended as an acknowledgment of our debt to these predecessors.[1] Though a few early examples will be offered, we will attempt no comprehensive survey of the entire literature, but instead we will emphasize five strands in the literature that are most pertinent to our work: (1) the multiplicity of equilibria that arise when there are scale economies or the costs of entry are substantial, (2) the tendency of the presence of scale economies to result in provision of any product by only a single supplier, (3) the effects of productivity growth in one country in classical models without scale economies, (4) the absence of certainty that the market mechanism will select among the set of potential equilibria one that is (or approximates) the social optimum, and (5) the structure of the formal models.

10.1   Scale Economies, Entry Costs and Multiple Equilibria

More than half a century ago, A. C. Pigou was among the first to explore the policy implications of multiple equilibria. In his groundbreaking *Economics of Welfare* there is a chapter that focuses on the case where there is more than one potential equilibrium. After showing how start-up costs can generate a multiplicity of stable equilibria, he writes:

> Benefit might be secured by a *temporary* bounty [i.e., a subsidy] (or temporary protection) so arranged as to jerk the industrial system out of its present poise at a position of relative [i.e., local] maximum, and induce it to settle down again at the position of absolute maximum—the highest hill-top of all. This is the analytical basis of the argument for the *temporary* protection, or other encouragement of infant industries; and if the right infants are selected, the right amounts of protection accorded, and this protection removed again at the right time, the argument is perfectly valid. (1932, p. 141)[2]

In other words, Pigou emphasizes that where entry cost into an industry is substantial, more than just a single outcome is likely to be possible for the market mechanism. Moreover, some of the possible outcomes may be far inferior to the true optimum, "the highest hill-top of all." And since an inferior outcome is apt to be stable, government intervention may be helpful or even required to free the economy from such an undesirable equilibrium.

Recognition and systematic examination of the idea that trade models with scale economies are characterized by multiple equilibria probably was first provided by Alfred Marshall. He examined the subject carefully in one of his earliest writings (1879), a piece initially printed for private circulation. Copies were sent to leading economists in the United Kingdom and other countries, and key portions were reproduced in several books before the monograph was published and became generally available in 1930. The international trade portion of the essay is 28 pages long, of which 16 pages deal primarily with the case of multiple equilibria. Thus it is clear that the notion was not a passing thought nor one whose significance was unrecognized by the author.

His multiple-equilibrium discussion deals explicitly with international trade. Marshall's formal analysis is entirely geometric, and uses the now-familiar offer curve diagram as its tool. The analysis is consequently framed in terms of a two-country, two-good model. He shows that in the presence of scale economies, and only in this case, the offer curves can have several intersections. (Figures 10.1 and 10.2 reproduce Marshall's graphs for the two cases.) Figure 10.2 is the scale economies case. Marshall calls it the exceptional case, "in which an increase in the amount of wares which a country produces for exportation effects a very great diminution in the expenses at which she can produce them" (1879, pp. 5–6). In this graph we see the three equilibrium points, A, B, and C. Marshall argues that intersection B is an unstable equilibrium, while A and C are stable (see Marshall's arrows in his figures 8 and 9).

Marshall offers two interpretations of the scale economies case. One is the standard static concept entailing a negatively sloping average cost curve of the usual sort: "They would then represent a case in which the trade between the two countries could not grow up gradually; but could be carried on with profit to both if it were once started on a large scale by any external cause" (1879, p. 15). Marshall's other type of scale economies (like that described by Krugman and Venables 1992) entails

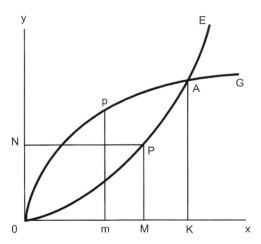

Figure 10.1
Marshall's two-country, two-good model (redrawn from the original)

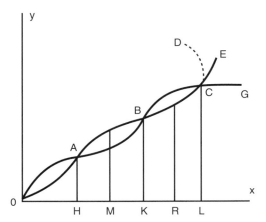

Figure 10.2
Marshall's scale economies model (redrawn from the original)

an introduction process that can require a substantial amount of time:
"The introduction of the economies which were requisite in order to
render possible such cases as this on a large scale have seldom been
effected within a short space of time. The lapse of generations has been
required for that development of England's invention and economies
in manufacture which was above attributed in part to her export trade.
... Special knowledge, special skill and special machinery are to a
greater or less extent required for the manufacture of these imple-
ments" (1879, pp. 13–14).

Moreover economies of this second type may be at least partly
irreversible:

[S]uppose that an increase in the amount of cloth produced for exportation
leads to the introduction of extensive economies. Such economies when they
have once been obtained are not readily lost. Developments of mechanical
appliances, of division of labor, and of organization of transport, when they
have once been effected are not readily abandoned. Capital and skilled labor
which have once been devoted to any particular industry, may indeed become
depreciated in value when there is a falling off in the demand for the wares
which they produce; but they cannot quickly be converted to other occupa-
tions." (1879, p. 27)

It is surely fair to associate this second type of scale economies with
the high cost of entry and the resulting retainability property that
underlies much of the discussion of this book.

Since Marshall, a number of writers have made valuable contributions and additions to the basic analysis of multiplicity of equilibria in

international trade (see, e.g., Matthews 1949–50; Meade 1952; Kemp 1964, 1969; Chipman 1965; Ethier 1979; Helpman and Krugman 1985, pp. 209–213; Krugman 1991; Krugman and Venables 1992; Romer 1994). The earlier of these discussions generally employed geometric methods of analysis, and therefore found it convenient to confine the study to the two-good, two-country case. Like Marshall, they also generally examined a situation involving a very small number (frequently three) equilibria. Apparently, we are the first to have shown (1992, 1994) that multiple equilibria do not merely exist but that they increase exponentially with the number of traded commodities, and that they constitute a region with robust qualitative characteristics and substantial economic implications.

It has also long been recognized that some of the multiple equilibria that result from scale economies and high entry costs can have undesirable welfare properties. It even led Frank Graham to argue as early as 1923 that permanent protection by a country of an industry that excludes imports of that industry's products altogether can sometimes be advantageous to the country that does so.[3] Marshall himself did not discuss the implications of multiple equilibria for the workings of the market mechanism and the reliability of the market's promotion of economic efficiency and the general welfare. This task was left to his successor, A.C. Pigou. We have already seen in the quotation from his *Economics of Welfare* earlier in this section how effectively he carried out that task. Pigou noted that where equilibrium is not unique market forces may well lead the economy to a local optimum that is far inferior (from the point of view of one, or more, or even all of the affected parties) to the true global maximum. He also noted that in such circumstances the public sector can play a useful role in improving the results yielded by the market mechanism, with either temporary or permanent intervention conceivably serving this purpose (*Economics of Welfare*, 4th ed., ch. 3, esp. p. 141). Thus Pigou clearly anticipated the general directions of our policy discussion.

The importance of multiple equilibria has also been clear to more recent writers: "The most interesting consequence of external economies is the existence of multiple equilibria," wrote John Chipman in 1965 (p. 749). But where such a multiplicity of candidate equilibria are present the market loses the manifest destiny to which a unique equilibrium would force it. There are then a number of possible end points, and as Graham pointed out three-quarters of a century ago, many of these equilibria can be quite undesirable, at least for one of the trading countries. Moreover, as Paul Romer (1994, p. 6) put it, in such circumstances, "We are forced to admit that the world as we know it is the result of a long string of chance outcomes." Paul Krugman (1991, p. 652) adds, "Once one has multiple equilibria, however, there is an obvious question: which equilibrium actually gets established? . . . On the one side there is the belief that the choice among multiple equilibria is essentially resolved by *history*: that past events set the preconditions that drive the economy to one or another steady state. . . . On the other side, however, is the view that the key determinant of choice of equilibrium is *expectations*."

Another branch of the literature, that focussed on innovation rather than international trade, has also emphasized that multiple equilibria can give historical accident an important role in the determination of the allocation of productive activities among countries (e.g., see David 1985, and the various recent writings of Brian Arthur, e.g., 1989). This analysis, too, raises the possibility that the market mechanism may conceivably lead to outcomes that do not most effectively promote the public interest, and that some of those outcomes may be at least partially irreversible, all of this implying that such considerations can open a useful economic role for government.

We see, then, that Krugman's remark—"In the emerging literature on increasing returns and externalities, multiple equilibria are not a nuisance but a central part of the story"—is clearly justified (1991, pp. 651–52).

10.2   Scale Economies and Tendency to Single Suppliers (Perfectly Specialized Equilibrium)

We have made extensive use in this book of the case of perfectly specialized equilibria because, among other reasons, scale economies tend to elicit assignments in which any particular commodity is provided by only a single supplier. Since we are concerned with entire economies rather than single firms, in our discussion "single supplier" means exclusive production of the item in question within a single country, but it does not necessarily imply that the item is supplied by a monopoly firm. Nevertheless, the argument associating scale economies with production within a single economy is the same as the standard "natural monopoly" analysis that associates scale economies with supply of a good or service by a single enterprise.

As Viner often emphasized to one of us, the search for the first writer to have produced any particular idea is a hunt for a chimera. Whenever a particularly early reference is discovered, it only serves to set off attempts to find earlier references, usually a bit less sophisticated but arguably on the point. Thus we will cite Cournot (1838, p. 76 of the English translation) as the author of a relatively early statement recognizing the incompatibility of scale economies and competition.[4]

The notion of "natural monopoly" seems to have been originated by J. S. Mill, though he only hints at its connection with scale economies:

All the natural monopolies (meaning thereby those which are created by circumstances, and not by law) which produce or aggravate the disparities in the remuneration of different kinds of labor, operate similarly between different employments of capital. If a business can only be advantageously carried on by a large capital, this in most countries limits so narrowly the class of persons who can enter into the employment, that they are enabled to keep their rate of profit above the general level. (*Principles of Economics*, bk. II, ch. 15, p. 394).

There is probably no way to trace the origin of the observation that equilibrium under scale economies tends to entail single-source supply. The idea is that where several suppliers coexist, the arrangement can be expected to be unstable because any supplier in such an initial state that succeeds in expanding its relative output will be able to underprice its rivals. This idea seems so obvious that it probably occurred to relatively early observers. Certainly Marshall and F. Y. Edgeworth treat the observation as a commonplace that hardly merits discussion. Though Marshall clearly devoted considerable space to his analyses of monopoly and economies of scale (both internal and external[5]), he seems only to have referred to our issue in one footnote. And there he treated it as a fairly clear-cut matter that some earlier writers had inexplicably overlooked:

Some, among whom Cournot himself is to be counted, have before them what is in effect the supply schedule of an individual firm; representing that an increase in its output gives it command over so great internal economies as much to diminish its expenses of production; and they follow their mathematics boldly, but apparently without noticing that their premises lead inevitably to the conclusion that, whatever firm first gets a good start will obtain a monopoly of the whole business of its trade in its district." (*Principles*, p. 459, fn)

Similarly, while no mention of the subject occurs in Edgeworth's noted article, "The Pure Theory of Monopoly" (1896) or in "The Laws of Increasing and Diminishing Returns" (1911, both reprinted in *Papers*

I), he covers the issue in one sentence in a book review of 1905: "The liability of an industry to be monopolized when it obeys the law of increasing returns creates peculiar difficulty in the application of the geometrical method to supply" (*Papers* III, p. 141).

Wicksell treats the subject with equal brevity (*Lectures*, pp. 131 and 233). He tells us: "If . . . the law of increasing returns applies without qualification. . . . The whole industry will be dominated by a more or less completely monopolistic association and all smaller concerns will disappear. . . . any attempt on the part of the smaller enterprise at effective competition . . . would be fruitless. . . . (p. 131).

Frank Knight (1924), too, emphasized the conflict between competition and scale economies, making it a central point in his criticism of Frank Graham's 1923 contention (see above) that under scale economies a country may well obtain losses rather than gains from trade.

Viner, in his justly noted article, "Cost Curves and Supply Curves," approaches the matter somewhat more extensively and in a different way:

The familiar proposition that net internal economies of large-scale production and long-run stable equilibrium are inconsistent under competitive conditions is clearly illustrated [by the cost-curve diagrams]. . . . [The firm] in short-run equilibrium when . . . its short-run marginal cost . . . is equal to price . . . will not be in long-run equilibrium, however, for its long-run marginal cost will then be . . . less than price.[6] Provided that no change in its output will affect market price, it will pay this concern to enlarge its plant whatever the price may be, and whatever its existing scale of plant may be. If thereby it grows so large that its operations exert a significant influence on price, we pass out of the realm of atomistic competition and approach that of partial monopoly. . . . (p. 40)

The subsequent evolution of the concept of "natural monopoly" is explored extensively by William Sharkey (1982). In any event, it is clear that the concept has since become a commonplace and is nowadays discussed at length in any volume on industrial organization or on the economics of regulation (e.g., see Kahn 1971, ch. 4, esp. pp. 116–123) and Kasserman and Mayo (1995, pp. 413–21). In more recent times Krugman has written extensively on the efects of economies of scale on international trade. His work has attracted considerable modern interest to the subject. We cite here one observation particularly pertinent to this book. Krugman and Venables tell us:

Then a country with a somewhat stronger initial position in some industry than its competitors may find itself with an advantage that cumulates over time.

Producers of final goods will find that the country with the larger industry supports a larger base of intermediate producers, which gives them low enough costs to export to other markets. . . . Thus, each industry will tend to concentrate in one of the countries . . . a dynamic process of regional specialization and differentiation. . . . (pp. 4–5)

Thus the notion that scale economies tend to lead to perfectly specialized equilibria[7] is widely recognized. Nevertheless, we should remind the reader that our analysis produces the same economic results when nonspecialized equilibria are included in the model.

10.3   Faster Productivity Growth in One Country in Models without Scale Economies

At least since 1953, after the noted Inaugural Lecture by J. R. Hicks, specialists in international trade have recognized that increases in the productivity of a lagging economy can sometimes decrease the overall welfare of a trading-partner country that is more advanced technologically. Nevertheless, debate on the subject has continued among economic historians (see, e.g., McCloskey 1981, pp. 133–83), and a substantial number of economists apparently still believe that such a productivity increase is either certain or very likely to be beneficial to both countries.

Our discussion of productivity follows the lead of the specialists, employing the same premises as they did to show, once again, that enhancement of productivity in one country can sometimes (but will not always) be harmful to another country. It also follows them in basing the analysis on Ricardian models whose trade equilibrium is shifted by improvements in productivity in one country or the other. However, we carry our analysis several important steps further. First, we focus on the effects of the productivity change upon total world output and the national income it provides to the two countries. We show that the previously unemphasized effects on world output, and the way in which they are shared among the trading countries, are at the heart of the issue. Our approach permits us to describe the full set of equilibria that correspond to the different productivity levels and to make a direct comparison of any pair of these equilibria in terms of their benefits to the world and to each of the trading countries. Second, our approach makes it possible to add to J. R. Hicks' generalization about the characteristics that determine whether in any particular case growth of productivity in country 2 is beneficial or detrimental to country 1.

In his Inaugural Lecture (1953) Professor Hicks sketched out an intuitive Ricardian model of the effect of increased productivity in country
2 on its own welfare and on that of its trading partner, country 1. He
concluded first that uniform increases in productivity in a trading
partner benefit both countries, and then went on to distinguish two
other cases. In the first case the improvements in country 2 are concentrated in its export industries, and his conclusion was that this
improvement is beneficial to both countries. The intuitive reason is
clear. Since country 2, which experiences technical progress in production of good X, is an exporter of X to country 1, the latter has no foreign
sales of X to lose as a result, and it can now purchase X more cheaply
than before.[8] In the second case discussed by Hicks, the improvements
are concentrated in country 2's import industries, and he concludes
that although this is good for country 2, country 1 is worse off. Intuitively this is so because some or all of its exports of X may then be
taken over by country 2, and/or the prices country 1 receives for those
exports will tend to fall.

Hicks's contribution was quickly followed by a number of expansions, formalizations and commentaries, including E. J. Mishan (1955),
H. G. Johnson (1955), W. M. Corden (1956), and Findlay and Grubert
(1959).

Hicks's fruitful line of thought was taken up again by Dornbush,
Fischer, and Samuelson (1977) in an explicit Ricardian model. This
groundbreaking paper is, perhaps, most noteworthy because of its
definitive break with the two-commodity models, presenting an inge-
nious graphic device that permits analysis of the extreme cases in
which the number of goods is infinite. On the subject we are now discussing, they concluded, like Hicks, that technological change spread
uniformly among the products of the improving country is good for
both countries. They also pointed out, however, that the international
transfer of technology from a high-wage country to a less advanced,
low-wage country can be harmful to the welfare of the transferring
country. In an illuminating paper that builds on the ideas of both
papers, Krugman (1985) took up the subject of trade between a technologically advanced country and its less advanced trading partner,
adding several pertinent and illuminating assumptions. He assumed
that the technologically advanced country was likely to make progress
more rapidly in its more technologically advanced sectors and traced
out the effect of this progress on both countries using a method of
analysis similar to that of Dornbush, Fischer, and Samuelson. He found

an interesting asymmetry. Progress in the advanced country is always beneficial to both countries, while progress in the less advanced country, while always beneficial to it, can, depending on circumstances, either be harmful or beneficial to the more advanced country. He pointed out that these results can be interpreted in terms of the tendency of the advanced country to make export-biased improvements and of the less advanced country to make improvements that are more import biased.

More recently Stafford et al. (Johnson and Stafford 1993, 1998; Hymans and Stafford 1995) have analyzed the effect of the improvement in a single industry in one of the countries. They found, consistent with the earlier work, that if the industry starts from a very low level of productivity, and the product is therefore entirely imported, the effects of an initial productivity increase in the low-productivity country, *if it affects trade*, are good for the improving country but harmful to the trading partner. However, at a later stage of productivity growth, when the industry is shifted entirely to the improving country, further improvements are beneficial to both. Whether the overall change yields a net gain or net loss to the other country depends on the balance of the two phases. To summarize, all this work offers the conclusion that productivity improvements in one country are always good (or, rather, never harmful) for it[9] but that the effect on its trading partner depends on the balance between the damaging effect on importing industries and the beneficial effect on exporting industries.

In this book we introduce different but complementary techniques that make it possible to ask and answer a different but complementary set of questions. Instead of looking at the effect of changes in productivity near an existing equilibrium,[10] we examine all possible productivity parameters and determine which sets of productivity parameters yield the best results for one country or for the other. It emerges, as we have seen, that the attributes that make another country the very best trading partner from the self-interested viewpoint of a developed country require that ideal trading partner to be the exporter of only a few products but to have very high productivity levels in the provision of those goods. This best outcome for the developed country is consequently usually a very poor one for its partly developed partner.

All these results require the presence of a reasonably substantial number (usually six or more) of industries, but then they are valid for all parameter choices, that is, for all models with a large number of products. Much of the previous literature has tended to deal either with models containing only two products or, at the other extreme (following the pathbreaking work of Dornbush, Fischer, and Samuelson), with an infinite number of products. It is easy to demonstrate that for our multiparameter analysis at least the model with two or three products behaves very differently from models with, say, six or more products. For example, in the case of a small number of products the interests of the trading partners are not characterized by the sources of conflict that always arise when the number of products is larger.

Our approach in this book also brings out a natural connection between this theory and one with economies of scale. The vast number of multiple equilibria that one generally finds in Ricardian models modified to entail economies of scale (see Gomory 1994) may be totally different from the linear-model equilibria that result as several industries are shifted from one country to the other by productivity changes. Nevertheless, all of these scale economies equilibria are included in the set of equilibria that are produced by our linear model if the range of parameter values in the latter is suitably wide. This introduces the tight connection, which we have called the *correspondence principle*, between the family of linear models with changing productivity levels and the results that are obtained from models with economies of scale. The implication is that there are behavioral attributes and policy consequences that carry over from the one case to the other, and that do not seem to have been observed before.

10.4   Governmental Promotion of Entry of an Economy into New Industries: Benefits, Costs, and Market Failure

One of the basic conclusions of our analysis is that entry into a new industry and acquisition of a substantial share of its world market is, in an apparently wide range of circumstances, beneficial to the country that succeeds in such an undertaking. Indeed, we suggest that it may sometimes be appropriate for government to encourage such a development. Obviously this analysis is not unrelated to the old infant industry argument, though we trust that the reader will find it carried out here on a more sophisticated level.

Viner tells us that: "Modern writers usually credit Alexander Hamilton or Friedrich List, or even John Stuart Mill, with the first presentation of the 'infant industry' argument for protection to young industries. It is of much earlier origin, however, and is closely related both in principle and in its history to the monopoly privileges granted to trading companies opening up new and hazardous trades and to inventions (the 'patents of monopoly')" (1937, p. 71). Yet, the passages cited by Viner, while clearly expressing the general idea, do not explore it nearly as thoroughly as Hamilton does, and thereby omit several features of the argument that are relevant to our analysis.[11]

Hamilton takes the position that protection of infant industries is called for primarily, but not exclusively, by the absence of complete freedom of international trade:

If the system of perfect liberty to industry and commerce were the prevailing system of nations, the arguments which dissuade a country, in the predicament of the United States, from the zealous pursuit of manufactures, would doubtless have great force. It will not be affirmed that they might not be permitted, with few exceptions, to serve as a rule of national conduct. In such a state of things, each country would have the full benefit of its peculiar advantages to compensate for its deficiencies or disadvantages. If one nation were in a condition to supply manufactured articles on better terms than another, that other might find an abundant indemnification in a superior capacity to furnish the produce of the soil. And a free exchange, mutually beneficial, of the commodities which each was able to supply, on the best terms, might be carried on between them, supporting, in full vigor, the industry of each. (*Report on Manufactures*, pp. 200–201)

Having gone on to point out that trade was hardly free (and having offered several supplementary arguments), Hamilton continues:

The spontaneous transition to new pursuits, in a community long habituated to different ones, may be expected to be attended with proportionably greater difficulty. . . . The apprehension of failing in new attempts is, perhaps, a more serious impediment. . . . To this it is of importance that the confidence of cautious, sagacious capitalists, both citizens and foreigners, should be excited. And to inspire this description of persons with confidence, it is essential that they should be made to see in any project which is new—and for that reason alone, if for no other, precarious—the prospect of such a degree of countenance and support from governments as may be capable of overcoming the obstacles inseparable from first experiments.

The superiority antecedently enjoyed by nations who have preoccupied and perfected a branch of industry, constitutes a more formidable obstacle than either of those which have been mentioned, to the introduction of the same branch into a country in which it did not before exist. To maintain, between the recent establishments of one country, and the long-matured establishments of another country, a competition upon equal terms, both as to quality and price, is, in most cases, impracticable. The disparity, in the one, or in the other, or in both, must necessarily be so considerable, as to forbid a successful rivalship, without the extraordinary aid and protection of government. (pp. 204–205)

According to Pigou (1906, p. 15), Colbert described protective duties as the "crutches to teach the new manufactures to walk" (no source given by Pigou). But Hamilton went well beyond this, citing fear of the unknown, response to unknown risks by the capital market, and the advantages of having gotten there first as primary reasons why market forces cannot ensure the discontinuous leaps necessary to bring an economy from an inferior equilibrium to one that serves its interests better.

There is no need to reproduce in any detail the similar arguments of Friedrich List[12] (1841; see also 1885, p. 300) or those of J. S. Mill (bk. V, ch. X, p. 423). It is only worth noting their common emphasis, in Mill's words, upon the possibility that: "The superiority of one country over another in a branch of production, often arises only from having begun it sooner. There may be no inherent advantage on one part, or disadvantage on the other, but only a present superiority of acquired skill and experience."

Moreover all these discussions focus on high start-up costs rather than on static economies of scale, and consider those costs to result from lack of experience in the prospective new industries, fear of uncertainty, capital market limitations, and other sources of high start-up costs as reasons why automatic market forces may perform imperfectly in the presence of multiple equilibria. Of course, the modern term "multiple equilibria" is never used, but the idea of the entry of an economy into an industry new to it is patently the same as the move from one such equilibrium to another.

The modern trade literature, with its repeated discussion of nonuniqueness of trade equilibria in the presence of scale economies, clearly implies that the move from one such equilibrium to another may be able to benefit a country. However, the issue seems only to have been reraised explicitly by Graham (1923). As already noted, Graham argued that if a country has a comparative disadvantage in an industry subject to scale economies, it may nevertheless be advantageous to it to prevent importation of that commodity and produce the item entirely domestically. Wilfred Ethier (1982) provides a careful formal analysis of the issue that seems to be accepted as the resolution of the discussion.

Recently a number of economists have begun to express more policy-oriented reservations about unrestricted free trade. The Spencer-Brander (1983) article has led to an extended and illuminating discussion (see also Tyson 1992).

A more general investigation of the advantages and disadvantages to the countries involved of the move to a new equilibrium through changes in the productivity performance of one of these trading partners has appeared recently in three pathbreaking papers (e.g., Johnson and Stafford 1993). These have already been summarized here and in chapter 4, and we will not repeat the discussion here. We need only conclude that in the area under consideration—the possibility of welfare gains through moves from one equilibrium to another and the obstacles to achievement of such gains by the unaided market mechanism—our discussion also owes much to earlier writers.

10.5 Relation to Other Scale Economies Models

Finally, we examine where our model fits in with the models employed elsewhere in the literature. The previous trade literature has emphasized three different variants of industry scale economies. While each corresponds to real and probably significant phenomena, they require markedly different analytic methods and yield very different conclusions (e.g., see Krugman 1984, pp. 109–110).

One set of widely used models of scale economies assumes them to be internal to the firm. As we have noted, this leads us to expect markets to be monopolistic or subject to monopolistic competition, and unless the markets are perfectly contestable, it is likely to entail nonzero profits.[13] Helpman, Grossman, and Krugman have been the pioneers in the use of this approach, and have produced entirely new, fundamental and extremely illuminating results with its aid (e.g., see Krugman 1979; Helpman 1984; Helpman and Krugman 1985; Grossman and Helpman 1991).

The second of the previously studied scale economies models entails worldwide externalities in which every producer firm in an industry benefits from the expansion of other firms in the industry, no matter in what countries they may be located. Though this situation was investigated by eminent scholars including Viner (1937), Ethier (1979), and Helpman and Krugman (1985), we will not discuss it further here because it goes in a direction so very different from ours.

The third group of models, with which the analysis in this book can be associated, is perhaps the most traditional in the literature. It assumes that firms are perfectly competitive, that they operate under constant or diminishing returns to scale, but that industry scale economies are produced by externalities that depend on the geographic proximity of the firms in question. Scale economies therefore benefit the firms within an industry only in a given country. Competition then will, of course, drive profits to zero. Examples of the many writings using this approach include Kemp (1969) and Ethier (1982). The concept goes back to Marshall's *Principles*. (For a good review of the history, see Chipman 1965, p. 740 ff). Our model is associated with this third group because we too assume that profits are zero despite the presence of scale economies.[14]

Though this is probably the most widely used of the scale economies constructs, it has always aroused controversy. It is sometimes suggested that this case rarely arises except where specialized labor is most effectively trained by experience on the job and the labor force is immobile internationally. There are many more cases, however, in which proximity generates economies external to the firm because the activities of one firm lend support to those of others. The modern semiconductor industry or, indeed, any complex manufacturing industry, is dependent on a host of specialized and experienced suppliers, especially of services, whose absence greatly complicates the startup of an industry and whose presence contributes greatly to efficiency. In such cases high start-up costs can indeed yield a range of ex ante scale economies for the industry, and yet entail constant returns for the firm, effective competition and, hence, a tendency to zero economic profits.

10.6 On Analytical Tools

Obviously some of the methods we have employed here are new. So far as we have been able to determine, the concept of the region of equilibrium points and its depiction in our basic graph have never been used before. Consequently the shape of that region and its economic implications have not been studied earlier. Nor has there previously been a calculation of the number of specialized equilibrium points and the rapidity of the growth of that number as a function of the number of traded commodities.

There have, however, clearly been predecessors in dealing, first, with the number of traded commodities and, second, with the effects on equilibrium of changes in parameter values, that is, in terms of comparative statics. Here, as will be shown in this section, while the literature plainly provides very powerful tools for comparative statics analysis, most of these tools permit only the study of local variations in parameters, that is, the effects of minuscule changes in their values. An exception to this is the work of Frank Stafford and his collaborators described in chapter 8. Our comparative statics analysis, in contrast, can be considered global, since it can deal with changes in parameter values of any feasible magnitude. This can be important because, as we have seen here, the qualitative character of the effects of small changes can be extremely different from those of more substantial variations.

Turning, first, to the number of traded commodities in a model, it has already been noted that almost all studies of trade in the scale economies case had, until the second half of the 1970s, considered worlds with only two traded goods. These studies were able to show that even with two goods, scale economies introduce multiple equilibria of which more than one can be stable, and some of which may not maximize welfare (e.g., see Matthews 1949–50; Meade 1952; Kemp 1969; Ethier 1979.) Then Dornbush, Fischer, and Samuelson achieved a major breakthrough in providing a procedure that deals with an infinite number of commodities. Since then, Helpman and Krugman (1985) and Grossman and Helpman (1991) have effectively incorporated into their analyses trade in n commodities, with the number n unspecified. Thus our use of n traded goods has a number of eminent predecessors.

However, so far as we know, no previous study has investigated the effect of the number of traded goods on the number and properties of the equilibria. We have demonstrated that the number of specialized equilibria in the two-country case grows as $2^n - 2$. More important, we have shown that things that can be true in the two-good case are generally very different when the number of traded goods is larger than, perhaps, a half-dozen. For example, in most of our discussion we have seen that the peak of country 1's region of equilibria is generally to the right of that of country 2, leading to the zone of conflict that we have repeatedly discussed. It can be shown, however, that in the two-good case these two peaks tend to coincide, so a two-good analysis is likely to overlook the zone of conflict and its significance for theory and policy.

There is no need to repeat here the earlier history of formal comparative statics analysis, going back at least to Cournot (1838), carried out more fully by Hicks and Allen (1934) and others, and then facilitated by Samuelson (1953) and others through use of revealed preference analysis and duality theory (introduced by Roy 1942 and others). The rather evident point here is that these analyses are all carried out with the aid of the differential calculus, and generally end up finding the partial derivative of some endogenous variable with respect to the value of one of the model's parameters (for an abundance of clear examples in trade theory, e.g., see Dixit and Norman 1980). Clearly, such a derivative can, by its very nature, describe only very local changes and responses. Our model, in contrast, lays out the entire region of equilibrium points and thereby brings out the full set of possible changes and responses, both local and global. This is patently critical in a model of scale economies where the uniqueness ensured by the appropriate convexity-concavity conditions is typically violated. So, as Pigou pointed out (see above), a move in the uphill direction can easily bring the economy further away from the true global maximum.[15] Moreover we have seen that while in some regions of our graph a local move will certainly be advantageous to both trading countries, this is emphatically not generally true of larger displacements. Thus here, as elsewhere in this book, we clearly owe a great debt to our predecessors. But we can also claim that building on their work, we have gone some steps further.

10.7   Concluding Remarks: Application to Discussions of Policy

The implications of scale economies, high costs of entry into an industry and multiplicity of equilibria for the role of government, and unrestricted freedom of trade are all part of a subject very much under current discussion. Once more, Krugman is a main contributor to this analysis (e.g., see Krugman 1983, 1984, 1987; Krugman and Lawrence 1993). Other noteworthy examples appear in Chichilnisky and Heal (1986). There is good reason to expect the debate to continue and expand, as international negotiations, influenced by nationalistic political pressures, keep the subject to the fore.

   In closing, we would like to point out that both of our analyses in this book are entirely within the realm of free trade. In our analysis of models with economies of scale, we only discussed free trade outcomes. But we pointed out that there were a vast range of possible free trade outcomes, all of which tend to be sustained by market forces. So that free trade, in the presence of retainable industries, tends to preserve what is, rather than move the world toward any one prede-termined outcome.

In our analysis of the effect of different productivity parameters, we considered the wide range of productivity parameters that are possible for a country, and how the changes in these parameters affected the countries national incomes. However, once again, we were discussing alternatives that might be available to a country, each of which was a free trade outcome. For each choice of parameter values it was the free trade equilibrium that we found and that we disussed. The effects we described, the ups and downs of the different national incomes that resulted from those parameter choices, these were all comparisons between outcomes, each of which was the result of free trade. Free trade, here too, allows a vast range of possible outcomes.

11

Empirical Evidence: The Persistence of Specialization in Industrialized Countries

Edward N. Wolff

There is no obvious way to test directly the models and analyses of the preceding chapters. Because history in a multiequilibrium world can select only one among the many candidate equilibria, none of the others will be more than potential outcomes that might have been, but in fact never were. There is of course no way that one can observe directly a state of affairs that was a possible prospect but that never actually occurred. Yet indirect tests of theoretical propositions are possible and legitimate. Their most common form takes predictions that emerge from a model under investigation, predictions different from those of alternative models, and seeks to determine whether these predictions are confirmed by reality. That is the approach adopted in this chapter, which focuses on trade patterns in manufactured goods.

Several of the previous chapters have emphasized the role of increasing internal returns to scale (IIRS) and learning-by-doing in the formation of comparative advantage. Here the word "internal" means that the effect occurs within an individual country in which production of the commodity in question takes place. The analysis in the preceding chapters suggests that economies of scale and/or high start-up costs lead different countries to specialize in different sets of products. A country that enters a new field or new product line early may be among a few countries able to dominate that line. It can do so by increasing production to the point at which costs are so low that potential additional competitors are unable to enter the field successfully (at least, without significant product or process innovation or sufficient support from their government). Even more important, a handicap to entry is the necessary accumulation of specialized knowledge that is acquired easily only by prior participation in the industry through "learning-by-doing" (see Arrow 1962). The resulting leadership positions may persist for long periods of time. The identity of the industries in which a country specializes may depend on history and a variety of particular influences, some of them fortuitous such as the availability or unavailability of ancillary industries that can substantially facilitate a country's success in the production of some particular product or type of products. This all suggests that positions of national leadership are likely to persist for long periods of time and ensure relatively stable patterns of industry specialization, the prime result being retainability.

It is helpful to contrast this line of argument with that of the Heckscher-Ohlin model and its factor-price equalization implications. In that model, trade specialization is taken to depend on relative abundance of the different factors of production. In cases where the Heckscher-Ohlin model entails factor-price equalization, it yields very sharp predictions about cross-country patterns in labor and total factor productivity (TFP) in an industry. Specifically it implies that productivity will be the same in all countries. If this is so and factor prices (i.e., wages and profit rates) are equalized among countries, then the choice of the industries in which a country specializes can depend only on the relative abundance of its different factors—whether it has relatively more labor, capital, or land than its competitors.[1]

Earlier work by Dollar and Wolff (1993) reported a marked convergence of labor productivity, capital–labor ratios, and TFP in the aggregate among developed economies in the post–World War II. A similar convergence has occurred at the industry level, though it is weaker for capital intensity than for labor productivity or TFP. In such circumstances a Heckscher-Ohlin type of model predicts that convergence in aggregate capital–labor ratios should be accompanied by convergence in the production patterns of these countries.

This chapter investigates whether there has been movement toward convergence in production patterns among industrialized OECD countries between 1970 and 1993. A trend toward convergence in product lines would lend support to the Heckscher-Ohlin class of models. However, since it is found, instead, that there has been little or no convergence in patterns of specialization among these countries, despite the convergence in aggregate productivity and relative factor abundance, the results tend to lend support to the economies of scale models of this book. In other words, the results suggest that trade in manufactures is characterized by a considerable degree of retainability.

11.1   Convergence of Production Patterns?

The issue to be investigated is whether the industrial production patterns of developed countries have tended toward convergence. To investigate this issue, we use the 1994 OECD Structural Analysis (STAN) industrial database, which covers 1970 to 1993. STAN provides statistics on value added, measured in both current and 1985 local prices, for 33 manufacturing industries. The STAN database has relatively complete data on fourteen OECD countries—Australia, Belgium, Canada, Denmark, Finland, France, Germany, Italy, Japan, the Netherlands, Norway, Sweden, the United Kingdom, and the United States.

For an indicator of specialization we chose the share of the total world production of a given commodity made in an individual country relative to its share of world GDP. We call this measure of relative production share "$RELPSHR_i^h$", an acronym that connotes the relative share of country h in the production of good I, valued in 1985 U.S. dollars.[2] The totals are made up of data from the fourteen STAN countries. RELPSHR is a fraction whose numerator is country h's share of the total production of product I among the fourteen countries, while the denominator measures country h's share of total GDP for these countries. Thus a value of RELPSHR greater than 1 means that country h's share of the group's total production of product I is higher than its share of the total GDP of this group, and a value less than 1 means that the country's share of production is lower than its share of GDP. RELPSHR tells us in which product lines a country's production is concentrated, that is, in which goods it specializes. In general, for each country some values of RELPSHR for a country will be greater than 1, and some will be less than 1.[3]

We chose thirty-three industries at the lowest level of aggregation for which the requisite data were available. They are all three-digit ISIC (International Standard Industrial Classification) industries, with the exception of transport equipment, for which information is available at the four-digit level. We divided the industries into three technology groups based on their average R&D intensity[4] of production in the OECD countries in 1985: low-tech (in which R&D intensity was less than 0.5 times the mean), medium-tech (those with 0.5 to 1.5 times the mean R&D intensity), and high-tech (with more than 1.5 times the mean R&D intensity).

Our investigation revealed that in the earliest year studied, 1970, Germany accounted for 14 percent of total manufactures for this group of countries, Japan 13 percent, and the United States 40 percent. In other words, these three countries together produced two-thirds of the total manufactures of the fourteen OECD countries. Germany's share of total manufacturing was considerably greater than its share of the fourteen-country GDP (14 percent vs. 9 percent), for a RELPSHR index of 1.48. Japan's share of manufactures was almost identical to its GDP share (13 percent), for a RELPSHR of 1.01. The U.S. manufacturing share was smaller (40 percent vs. 45 percent), yielding a RELPSHR value of 0.89 (table 11.1 reports these results).

Germany's production in 1970 was heavily specialized in beverages, petroleum refineries, petroleum and coal products, industrial chemicals, motor vehicles, electrical machinery, and professional goods and scientific instruments (all with values of RELPSHR exceeding 1.8). Japan in 1970 was particularly strong in plastics, glass and glass products, and other transport equipment (all values above 1.6). America's major specialization was aircraft (a value of 1.7).

In 1970 Germany led all countries in relative share of total manufacturing, in all the high-tech industries except aircraft, in motor vehicles, and in seven of the low-tech industries as well. Italy led in five industries, including textiles, wearing apparel, footwear, and motorcycles and bicycles. Japan was the leader in only one industry (food products), the United States in only one (aircraft), Belgium in three (including industrial chemicals), Sweden in one (wood products), Finland in one (paper and paper products), Norway in two (including shipbuilding), Australia in two (including railroad equipment), and Denmark, the Netherlands, and the United Kingdom each in one.

A little more than two decades later, both Germany's and America's share of total manufacturing production had declined by three percentage points, but Japan's had increased by a dramatic ten percentage points. In fact, by 1993, Japan's manufacturing output was more than double Germany's and over 60 percent of the level of the United States. By 1993 Japan had the highest value of RELPSHR in total manufacturing (an index of 1.27), Germany's RELPSHR score had fallen to 1.22, while the U.S. value remained at 0.89.

In 1993 Germany remained extremely specialized only in petroleum refineries and motor vehicles (values of RELPSHR exceeding 1.8), with the United States very specialized only in aircraft (a value of 1.76). Japan, though, was now highly specialized in a number of industries: iron and steel, shipbuilding, motor vehicles, motorcycles and bicycles, other transport equipment, and, especially, electrical machinery (all values above 1.6). By 1993 Japan was the leading country in total man-ufacturing, and the leader in two high-tech industries (nonelectrical machinery and electrical machinery), as well as other manufactures. Italy led in eight industries; the United Kingdom and Germany in three; the Netherlands, Finland, Belgium, and Australia in two; and Sweden, France, Denmark, Canada, Norway, and the United States in just one apiece.

The last part of table 11.1 shows the correlation (and rank correla-tion) between the distribution of relative production shares among the three countries. What is striking is the low correlation among the three countries. In 1970, the correlation coefficient was 0.07 between Germany and the United States, −0.57 between Japan and the United States, and −0.33 between Germany and Japan. The rank correlations are similar. Between 1970 and 1993, the correlation coefficient (and the rank correlation) between Germany and the United States turned slightly negative and remained negative between Japan and the United States and between Germany and Japan, though its absolute value declined. Clearly, the three countries have specialized in distinctly dif-ferent industries and there has been very little change over time in the dissimilarity of their patterns of specialization.

11.2   Trends in Cross-country Dispersion

We turned next to an investigation of what has happened to the cross-country dispersion in the RELPSHR measures. The last two columns of table 11.1 show the coefficient of variation among countries for each industry in 1970 and 1993. There was no clear trend over this period: Between 1970 and 1993 dispersion increased in 13 industries and decreased in 10 industries in the low-tech group, increased in 4 and fell in 1 in the medium-tech group, and rose in 1 but declined in 4 in the high-tech group. The biggest changes spanned the range of low-tech to high-tech industries: textiles (0.55 to 0.93), footwear (0.77 to 1.50), plas-tics (0.67 to 0.31), shipbuilding (1.06 to 0.62), electrical machinery (0.41 to 0.70), and professional goods (1.01 to 0.68). By 1993 the most spe-cialized industries were tobacco products, textiles, leather products, footwear, pottery and china, motorcycles and bicycles, other transport equipment, and aircraft (all with coefficients of variation exceeding 0.9). The most diversified industries were food, beverages, printing and publishing, plastics, nonmetal products, metal products, other chemi-cal products, and nonelectrical machinery (all with coefficients of

Table 11.1
Relative production shares (RELPSHR) of Germany, Japan, and the U.S.; the OECD leader; and the coefficient of variation of RELPSHR among the 14 OECD countries, 1970 and 1993[a]

Industry	1970				1993				Coefficient of Variation[b]	
	GER	JPN	USA	Leader	GER	JPN	USA	Leader	1970	1993
Total manufacturing	1.48	1.01	0.89	GER	1.22	1.27	0.89	JPN	0.18	0.21
Low-tech industries[c]										
Food	0.93	1.56	0.67	JPN	0.84	1.16	0.78	DNK	0.24	0.29
Beverages	2.15	1.51	0.44	GER	1.62	0.82	0.61	UK	0.37	0.39
Tobacco	2.62	0.18	1.12	GER	3.94	0.24	0.70	NET	0.81	1.05
Textiles	1.23	1.25	0.63	ITA	0.86	0.68	0.86	ITA	0.55	0.93
Wearing apparel	1.26	1.08	0.81	ITA	0.55	1.04	0.97	ITA	0.31	0.65
Leather and products	1.47	1.15	0.48	BEL	0.86	1.12	0.48	ITA	0.74	1.04
Footwear	1.30	0.25	0.74	ITA	0.68	0.27	0.39	ITA	0.77	1.50
Wood Products	0.94	0.81	1.08	SWE	0.86	0.59	1.23	SWE	0.61	0.56
Furniture and fixtures	1.84	1.21	0.71	GER	1.31	0.85	0.82	ITA	0.27	0.48
Paper and products	0.99	0.80	1.06	FIN	0.96	0.88	1.09	FIN	0.76	0.89
Printing and publishing	0.62	1.45	1.01	NOR	0.53	1.15	0.98	UK	0.34	0.27
Petroleum Refineries	2.98	0.47	0.67	GER	2.30	0.67	0.60	FRA	1.04	0.80
Petroleum and coal	2.37	0.39	1.10	GER	1.66	0.52	1.27	NET	0.77	0.63
Rubber Products	1.68	0.73	0.94	GER	0.94	1.12	0.95	ITA	0.44	0.41
Plastic Products	1.28	1.72	0.74	AUS	1.31	1.31	0.92	GER	0.67	0.31
Pottery and china	1.22	1.19	0.74	ITA	0.88	1.01	0.28	ITA	0.97	1.28
Glass and products	1.11	1.65	0.91	BEL	1.56	1.03	0.75	BEL	0.59	0.70
Nonmetal products	1.58	1.27	0.65	DNK	1.50	1.22	0.69	AUS	0.28	0.36
Iron and steel	1.67	1.28	1.00	GER	1.71	1.66	0.72	GER	0.51	0.44

Nonferrous metals	1.25	1.28	1.01	NOR	1.65	1.41	0.70	NOR	0.64	0.58
Metal products	1.63	0.76	0.85	ITA	1.69	1.02	0.89	GER	0.42	0.36
Shipbuilding[h]	0.54	1.26	0.77	NOR	0.72	1.73	0.71	FIN	1.06	0.62
Other manufactures	0.66	1.59	0.87	UK	0.40	2.46	0.71	JPN	0.67	0.83
Medium-tech industries[c]										
Industrial Chemicals	2.07	0.89	0.84	BEL	1.49	0.96	0.88	BEL	0.52	0.72
Railroad Equipment[h]	0.43	0.48	0.44	AUS	0.54	0.71	0.49	AUS	0.86	0.67
Motor Vehicles[h]	1.83	1.38	0.85	GER	1.82	1.64	0.76	GER	0.61	0.75
Motorcycles and Bikes[h]	0.68	1.48	0.35	ITA	0.66	1.68	0.30	ITA	0.98	1.22
Other Transp. Equip.[h]	1.15	2.07	0.00	NET	1.03	2.20	0.00	CAN	0.90	1.16
High-tech industries[c]										
Chemical products[d]	1.57	0.85	1.09	GER	1.19	1.13	1.03	GER	0.36	0.29
Nonelectrical machinery[e]	1.74	0.93	0.86	GER	1.10	1.21	1.09	JPN	0.41	0.31
Electrical machinery[f]	1.86	0.19	1.11	GER	1.18	2.23	0.74	JPN	0.41	0.70
Aircraft[h]	0.30	0.11	1.66	USA	0.40	0.15	1.76	USA	0.96	0.91
Professional goods[g]	2.29	0.38	1.20	GER	1.35	0.66	1.34	UK	1.01	0.68

Correlations in relative production shares between:

	1970	1993
Germany and the United States	0.07	−0.06
Japan and the United States	−0.57	−0.42
Germany and Japan	−0.33	−0.23

Table 11.1 (continued)

Rank correlations in relative production shares between:

	1970	1993
Germany and the United States	0.17	−0.01
Japan and the United States	−0.49	−0.28
Germany and Japan	−0.34	−0.09

a. Relative production share of country h in industry I defined as:

$$RELPSHR_i^h = \frac{Y_i^h / \Sigma_h Y_i^h}{GDP^h / \Sigma_h GDP^h}$$

where the aggregation over h is based on 14 OECD countries with pertinent data: Australia (AUS), Belgium (BEL), Canada (CAN), Denmark (DNK), Finland (FIN), France (FRA), Germany (GER), Italy (ITA), Japan (JPN), the Netherlands (NET), Norway (NOR), Sweden (SWE), the United Kingdom (UK), and the United States (USA).

b. The coefficient of variation is defined as the ratio of the standard deviation to the (unweighted) mean.

c. Division of industries into technology groups is based on the average R&D intensity of production of OECD countries in 1985, as follows: low-tech—less than 0.5 times the mean R&D intensity; medium-tech—from 0.5 to 1.5 the mean R&D intensity; and high-tech—over 1.5 the mean R&D intensity.

d. Includes drugs and medicines and other chemicals.

e. Includes office and computing machinery and machinery and equipment.

f. Includes radio, TV and communication equipment and electrical apparatus.

g. Includes scientific instruments.

h. Calculations exclude Belgium.

variation less than 0.4). Here too both sets of industries run the gamut between low-tech and high-tech enterprises.

The finding that there was little change in the degree of specialization among manufacturing industries may be somewhat surprising in light of the evidence that aggregate measures of factor endowments (e.g., the capital–labor ratio for the entire economy) have become more similar in these advanced economies. On the other hand, the result is consistent with the finding that dispersion of productivity at the industry level remains high, and that there has been no strong trend toward cross-country convergence of industry-level productivity since the mid-1970s. It appears that countries are maintaining their specializations in different industries. Thus it is that aggregate productivity is converging among these countries, while at the same time industry-level productivity continues to diverge and production patterns are highly dispersed.

It is also striking that the specialization patterns of most countries persist over time. Table 11.2 shows correlation coefficients of the logarithm of RELPSHR values by industry within each country between 1970 and 1979 and between 1970 and 1993.[5] With only a few exceptions, these correlations remain very high over time. Between 1970 and 1979, the correlation coefficients are 0.88 or greater for all 14 countries, and between 1970 and 1993, they are 0.79 or higher for 10 of the 14 countries. The exceptions are Belgium, Japan, Sweden, and the United Kingdom (though, even for these four, the correlations exceed 0.60).

Rank correlations are also shown in table 11.2, and they are almost as strong for the period 1970 to 1979 as the correlations of LN(RELPSHR), exceeding 0.85 for all fourteen countries. However, rank correlations are weaker for the period 1970 to 1993 (exceeding 0.70 for ten countries), and fall in the range 0.58 to 0.69 for the other four countries (Finland, Japan, Sweden, and the United Kingdom). These results suggest that there was greater industrial restructuring in the 1980s than the 1970s.

Even though countries tend to retain the industries in which they specialize, over time it is still possible that they have become more alike in terms of the industrial composition of their output—that is, that they have moved closer to the average industrial composition of the fourteen countries used in the analysis here. This is a difficult issue to test formally. Table 11.2 (last two columns) uses the sum of squared values of LN(RELPSHR), where the summation is performed across industries

Table 11.2
Correlation over time in relative production shares (RELPSHR) by industry within country, 1970–1979 and 1970–1993, and the sum of squared values of RELPSHR, 1970 and 1993

Country	Correlation of the logarithm of relative production shares [LN(RELPSHR)]		Rank correlation of relative production shares (RELPSHR)		Summation of squared values of LN (RELPSHR)	
	1970–1979	1970–1993	1970–1979	1970–1993	1970	1993
Australia	0.97	0.85	0.94	0.73	31.9	31.2
Belgium[a]	0.88	0.75	0.86	0.73	22.5	20.6
Canada	0.98	0.93	0.95	0.85	42.9	41.8
Denmark	0.99	0.94	0.97	0.85	64.3	59.3
Finland	0.95	0.79	0.89	0.67	20.4	19.3
France	0.99	0.98	0.87	0.84	33.5	32.7
Germany	0.96	0.82	0.95	0.77	10.9	8.4
Italy	0.96	0.89	0.96	0.86	18.5	20.4
Japan	0.88	0.71	0.86	0.64	18.3	12.1
Netherlands	0.95	0.88	0.90	0.78	31.1	33.2
Norway	0.96	0.79	0.93	0.77	49.7	58.7
Sweden	0.95	0.64	0.92	0.58	13.1	18.6
United Kingdom	0.92	0.61	0.92	0.60	5.0	4.6
United States	0.98	0.95	0.93	0.70	20.4	21.2

Note: Correlations and sum of squared values are based on thirty-three industries unless otherwise indicated.
a. All industries except shipbuilding and repair, railroad equipment, motor vehicles, motorcycles and bicycles, other transport equipment, and aircraft.

within a country. This measure compares each country's relative industry production with the cross-country average relative production in a given industry.[6] If countries are becoming less specialized over time, then their production structure should be converging on the overall average of the countries, and this index should decline.

In 1970 Denmark was the most specialized country, according to this index, followed by Norway and Canada, and the United Kingdom was the least specialized. For our discussion, it is significant that these indexes remain relatively stable over time, with the notable exceptions of Japan (for which the index declines from 18.3 in 1970 to 12.1 in 1993), Norway (for which it rises from 49.7 to 58.7), and Sweden (from 13.4 to 18.6). However, what is most striking is that the total sum of squared values (summed across all countries) is almost identical in 1993 and 1970 (equaling approximately 382 in both years). This result again indicates that the degree of industry specialization among these fourteen countries has remained virtually unchanged over this twenty-three-year time span.

11.3   Patterns of Country Leadership in Industrial Sectors

Let us consider, finally, the stability of leadership in the different industrial sectors (see table 11.3). Does a country that attains a position of leading supplier of some product tend to retain that status, as in the situation upon which the analysis of this book focuses? In seeking to determine the answer statistically, we must reduce as far as possible the distorting influence of business cycle fluctuations. We therefore classify a country as a leader if it has the highest value in RELPSHR in at least three out of five consecutive years (or two consecutive years at the beginning or end of the data series). Germany, for example, led in terms of relative production share in total manufacturing from 1970 to 1991, when it was overtaken by Japan.

The noteworthy conclusion is that there was considerable stability in leadership in terms of relative production shares among the individual industries. Of the 33 industries in table 11.2, in 16 industries there was no change in country leader throughout the entire period, and there was only one change of leadership in 14 industries. In furniture and fixtures and plastic products, there were 2 changes of leadership, while in nonmetal products, there were 5 changes. It is also noteworthy that Germany, Japan, and the United States led in the high-tech industries, while, as the analysis of the book may suggest, leadership in the medium-tech industries was more spread out, among Belgium, Australia, Germany, Italy, the Netherlands, and Canada. Moreover, among the more interesting changes is the takeover in leadership position by Japan from Germany in the two high-tech industries, nonelectrical machinery (e.g., computers) and electrical machinery (e.g., radio, televisions, and communication equipment). These results on the general stability of leadership in production shares are in accord with those of table 11.2, which show a very high correlation over time in industry RELPSHR within the countries.

11.4   Concluding Remarks

In 1970 the world's major industrialized countries tended to specialize in very different manufacturing industries. Among the three largest

Table 11.3
Leadership and leadership changes in relative production share (RELPSHR) for 29 manufacturing industries, 1970–1993

	Leader (years)
Total manufacturing	GER (1970–91), JPN (1992–93)
Low-tech industries	
Food	JPN (1970–78), DNK (1979–93)
Beverages	GER (1970–82), UK (1983–93)
Tobacco	GER (1970–88), NET (1989–93)
Textiles	ITA (1970–93)
Wearing apparel	ITA (1970–93)
Leather and products	BEL (1970–74), ITA (1975–93)
Footwear	ITA (1970–93)
Wood products	SWE (1970–93)
Furniture and fixtures	GER (1970–75), BEL (1976–79), ITA (1980–93)
Paper and products	FIN (1970–93)
Printing and publishing	NOR (1970–78), FIN (1979–93)
Petroleum refineries	GER (1970–71), FRA (1972–93)
Petroleum and coal products	NOR (1970–77), NET (1978–93)
Rubber products	GER (1970–87), ITA (1988–93)
Plastic products, nec	AUS (1970–81), JPN (1982–87), GER (1988–93)
Pottery, china, etc.	ITA (1970–93)
Glass and products	BEL (1970–93)
Nonmetal products, nec	DNK (1970–73), GER (1974–76), DNK (1977–79), GER (1980–84), FIN (1985–87), AUS (1989–93)
Iron and steel	GER (1970–93)
Nonferrous metals	NOR (1970–93)
Metal products	ITA (1970–77), GER (1978–93)
Shipbuilding and repair	NOR (1970–81), FIN (1982–93)
Other manufactures nec	UK (1970–80), JPN (1981–93)
Medium-tech industries	
Industrial chemicals	BEL (1970–93)
Railroad equipment	AUS (1970–93)
Motor vehicles	GER (1970–93)
Motorcycles and bicycles	ITA (1970–93)
Other transport equipment	NET (1970–72), CAN (1973–93)
High-tech industries	
Other chemical products	GER (1970–93)
Nonelectrical machinery	GER (1970–89), JPN (1990–93)
Electrical machinery	GER (1970–83), JPN (1984–93)
Aircraft	USA (1970–93)
Professional goods	GER (1970–93)

Note: A country is considered a leader if it has the highest value in at least three out of five consecutive years.

economies—Germany, Japan, and the United States—the correlations (and rank correlations) in production shares by industry in 1970 are either negative or close to zero. There are also very low correlations in production shares between the United States and the other eleven OECD countries studied in the analysis. Moreover there was no tendency over time toward greater similarity in industries of specialization among the fourteen countries. A comparison of the coefficient of variation in relative production shares measured across countries within industry shows, on net, little change in the degree of specialization among manufacturing industries.

Most countries retained their pattern of specialization between 1970 and 1993. Correlation coefficients of the logarithm of RELPSHR by industry between 1970 and 1979 and between 1970 and 1993 are quite high for almost all of the countries. It is also noteworthy that there was considerable stability in leadership in terms of relative production shares among the individual industries. Of the thirty-three industries in the analysis, in sixteen industries there was no change in the country that led throughout the entire period, and there was only one change of leadership in fourteen industries. The general stability over time in the industries in which a country specialized is confirmed by the overall sum of squared values of the logarithm of RELPSHR within each country, which is almost identical in 1970 and 1993.

The general stability over time in the industries in which each country specialized lends support to the relevance of the models of this book and tends to raise some doubts about the pertinence of the Heckscher-Ohlin class of models or (presumably) the static classical model with costless entry and constant or diminishing returns to scale. The revised trade model in this book stresses the advantages of initial leadership in an industry and the consequent cost reduction emanating from increased production volume. In contrast, the Heckscher-Ohlin models suggest that specialization among the advanced countries should become less marked over time if their relative factor abundance converges, as it has in reality. The coefficient of variation in the overall capital–labor ratio (computed from the OECD International Sectoral Database, or ISDB) among these fourteen countries fell from 0.28 in 1970 to 0.17 in 1992. Despite this growing similarity in relative factor abundance, these countries tended to remain specialized in the same industries in 1993 as in 1970.

If industry specialization is influenced by the technology-related assets owned by the firm or embodied in technical labor, then investment in research and development and training of skilled labor are clearly important influences for the promotion of such specialization. And, if many of these assets really are industry specific, then it is likely that past history, as well as past and current government policy, will have a substantial effect on the kinds of assets accumulated and consequently on the industries that emerge as major producers. For instance, U.S. concentration of R&D in military-related industries clearly is a significant element in the explanation of the leading U.S. position in aircraft, large-scale computers, and advanced telecommunications. Japanese industrial policy, on the other hand, has directed R&D toward advanced consumer products such as automobiles and consumer electronics. Past history is also important for certain industries: Large German and U.S. firms that entered the chemical industry early continue to devote substantial resources to R&D in this industry and to maintain high production shares.

The bottom line of all this is that, according to the data, trade in manufactures shows patterns that we would expect of industries that are retainable—those dealt with in much of this book.

Notes

Preface

1. Angus Maddison, *Monitoring the World Economy 1820–1992*, Paris: OECD, 1995.

Chapter 1

1. Specialists have long been aware that reality is more complex than the world described in the most rudimentary accounts of the theory. There have been significant writings discussing such concepts as an optimal tariff (e.g., Scitovsky 1947), the valid elements in the infant industry argument, and the possibility that economic efficiency can be damaged by a customs union agreement among a set of countries, dropping trade barriers against one another but leaving those against other nations intact (Viner 1950). These analyses suggest that a move toward laissez faire may not always be the path to perfection.

2. On the role of scale economies in trade analysis, there is a rich body of relatively recent writings by Grossman and Helpman (1991), Helpman and Krugman (1985) and Ethier (1982). In that literature it is recognized that where scale economies are present, one can still legitimately retain a belief in the virtue of unrestricted freedom of trade but can no longer treat this as an open-and-shut matter. Rather, it is shown in these writings that in a world characterized by scale economies, a defensible free-trade position must be based on a balancing of the trade-offs the issue entails.

3. One aspect of global trade that has frequently been noted but that we do not discuss in this book is the growing internationalization of companies themselves. It will become clear, as the model we use is discussed in greater detail, that this phenomenon, though important in many other ways, does not substantially affect our analysis which focuses on the national and industry levels. For our purposes an oil refinery in the United States contributes the value of the goods it produces to the U.S. gross domestic product, whether or not it is part of an international oil company.

Chapter 2

1. The classical economists were, of course, intelligent individuals who observed reality and recognized that all was not always for the best in this best of all possible worlds. They knew that the economy had its shortcomings and its problems. Yet the assertion

that international trade, when guided by unrestrained competitive market forces, must yield a unique and generally beneficent outcome is not a serious distortion of the implications of their model, whose logic will be reviewed briefly in this chapter.

2. We include in the diminishing returns case the possibility that productivity neither increases nor decreases when the scale of production rises. This is the widely used linear model.

3. At the end of the eighteenth century more than 90 percent of the U.S. labor force is estimated to have worked on the land; today the figure is less than 3 percent.

4. To illustrate, assume first that there are only three products in the two-country world: transistors t, aerial navigation gyroscopes g, and cellular telephones c. Then the U.K. may specialize in any one of t, g, or c, leaving the remaining two to France. That already gives three possible equilibria. But there are also three possible equilibria in which France specializes in just one of the products. We see that with two products to be traded between two countries there are six equilibria, for example, the one in which the U.K. produces t and France produces g and c, the one in which the U.K. produces t and g and France produces c, and so on. In reality, of course, many more than three products are traded, and as the number of products in the model increases the number of equilibria grows far faster than the number of products, as table 2.1 indicates. We see that by the time the model is extended to include the production of ten commodities, the number of equilibria already exceeds one thousand.

After the number of traded products exceeds 20, the number of equilibria really takes off, exceeding 100 million in a 27-product world. Since in the real world the number of products with some substantial scale economies that enter into international trade undoubtedly is at least well into the thousands, it should be obvious that the large number of possible equilibria discussed here is no bit of science fiction.

Those readers who have studied the logic of combinations and permutations will recognize that we are discussing the number of combinations of n products that can be assigned to one or the other of two countries. Since each commodity can be assigned either to the U.K. or to France, the number of such combinations is 2^n. If we rule out the possibility of total exclusion of either country from the production of anything, the number of combinations becomes $2^n - 2$. This is the basic formula for the number of perfectly specialized equilibria on which many of the calculations in the next chapter are based.

Chapter 3

1. Our illustrative numbers are chosen to keep the arithmetic simple. Our numbers are much larger than the actual GDP figures for the two countries.

2. If we were to plot the nonspecialized equilibria, they too would lie under the upper boundary. However, some can lie below the lower boundary. These represent particularly poor outcomes.

3. Zero is possible because we are discussing, at this point, only the goods that are exchanged in international trade. But in addition to the goods and services that are exchanged in international trade and on which we focus here, there are others such as retailing, homebuilding, and so on, that are not traded. These provide an underpinning

for national income, whatever the division of the traded goods. We will discuss this and some related observations in chapter 9.

4. The U.K. position is represented by a dot in figure 3.3, while the French position in the same equilibrium is represented by a dot in figure 3.4; so where we combine them in figure 3.5 that equilibrium must still be represented by two dots, one for U.K. and one for France.

5. The U.K. peak, U, *must* always lie to the right of the French peak, F, because, as we have seen, U lies to the right of the world peak and F must lie to its left.

Chapter 4

1. Retainability and productivity change can also easily be combined, but the result, though more complicated, does not change the basic picture presented here.

2. Specialists will recognize that the discussion of this chapter applies equally to the more general case of diseconomies of scale, in which smaller firms have a cost advantage over large ones.

3. As sufficient time passes, productivity limits (i.e., the bounds of what is inherently possible) will also change. But at any given moment they are more or less fixed. In the mathematical models that underlie this discussion it is possible to vary the limits, but the substantive results, and in particular, the graphs that emerge, are the same as those discussed here. However, the economic interpretation of the results is enriched if the variability of the limits is taken into account, so we will return to this point later in the chapter.

4. Mathematical analysis shows that there can be small gaps just under the upper boundary curve. These gaps become smaller and smaller as more industries are included in the model. For models with 10 or more industries the gaps would scarcely be visible in a diagram of this size and could not affect our economic conclusions.

5. The same reasoning as in chapter 3 holds here: To the right of the world income peak, the world income "pie" starts to shrink in size, but since the U.K. share of it is rising as we move further to the right in the graph, the U.K. national income continues to rise. Eventually the effect reaches its limit, after which the rising U.K. share cannot offset the shrinking world income. Only then does U.K. income start to decline.

6. The mathematical analysis of this model and that of the retainable-industries model are in fact identical, and they lead to the same regional shape. The very close connection between the two models is discussed in chapter 8, where we describe what we call the correspondence theorem.

7. We are implicitly assuming that the industries are such that the maximum productivities of both countries are not too different. Note that we are discussing the manufacture of products such as athletic shoes, an acquirable skill, rather than, say, gold mining, which is difficult without gold in the ground.

8. In our analysis we can in fact allow the maximal productivities in an industry to increase. Then both countries can increase their productivities without changing their relative productivities, that is, their productivities compared to each other. As one might expect, in this case there is absolutely no change in the shapes of the regions in

our diagram. The boundaries are simply higher up, reflecting the higher productivity. Our economic conclusions, which depend only on shape, remain the same. This is in accord with both common sense and the usual view of economists. In a competitive situation it is the relative productivity of one country's industry compared to the other country's industry that makes one succeed and the other fail, and that has not changed.

Chapter 5

1. As our measure of income, we used Robert Summers and Alan Heston's *Penn World Table 5.6* with their extremely sophisticated estimates of per-capita real gross national product (GDP) for a group of 101 countries (for details, see Summers and Heston 1991). These data are for national incomes divided by the population of each country, with comparable statistics of per-capita income which are adjusted for inflation. To fit these comparisons with our two-country analysis, we can treat Western Europe as a single entity in its trade with the United States.

2. Japan's per-capita income also places it in the zone of conflict.

3. Our analysis has been carried out in terms of a world composed of only two countries. This patently unrealistic premise was adopted to simplify the analysis and its discussion. However, we show in chapter 9 that the analysis is also valid for the case of more than two countries.

4. There are, of course, many other things that differentiate potato chips from computer chips. For example, leadership in computer chips may provide some spillover effects that benefit other industries. The term "spillover effects" refers to benefits of or harm from an economic transaction that affect persons who are not direct participants in the transaction. However, here we are examining only differences that matter for our analysis, which, in its simplest form, assumes away any spillover effects.

5. The unsuccessful attempts to enter the flat panel display market are a recent example of the difficulty that the United States has in doing this.

6. Obviously, this tended to raise prices for U.S. consumers at least temporarily. Economists have consequently questioned the desirability of such "voluntary" acts, which, in effect, encourage foreign sellers to act like monopolists, restricting sales and raising prices.

7. According to a Lou Harris survey of 405 large companies in 1991, the greater the share of a firm's labor force outside the United States, the more likely it was to have downsized at home.

8. Charles E. Wilson, then chairman of General Motors, in testimony before the U.S. Senate Committee on the Armed Services, 1952.

9. In chapter 9 we show how the model can be modified to incorporate more features of the real world that were deliberately omitted from the discussion so far, for the sake of simplicity. These include industries in which a number of countries are producers; the role of (mostly) nontraded goods and services such as health care, housing construction and haircuts; and trade among more than two countries. It is encouraging that as we add more realism to the model, the economic conclusions we obtained from the original, simpler model persist unchanged.

Chapter 6

This chapter discusses some theoretical points arising from the materials in chapter 2 of part I.

1. Zero profit is, of course, assumed in the most traditional model of international trade, following Marshall's *Principles*, and since utilized by many others including Kemp (1969) and Ethier (1982). (For a review of the earlier literature based on this premise, see Chipman 1965, p. 740 ff). This model assumes that the economies are external to the firm but internal to the industry, and that they can be attributed to the private investment in infrastructure and ancillary activities that growth of the industry in question elicits. Our qualitative analysis, however, is not dependent on the zero-profit assumption, but it does facilitate the construction of a program for the calculation of the equilibrium points and the boundaries of the region of equilibrium points.

2. The reader may note that we do not explicitly include a balance-of-trade requirement for equilibrium, even though trade obviously cannot be in equilibrium if the value of imports is unequal to the value of exports. However, it is easily shown that if all of a country's income is spent on the purchase of commodities, a set of outputs and prices that satisfies our equilibrium conditions must automatically make the value of each country's exports equal to its imports: for then the value of the country's income, which, by definition, equals its domestic sales of its domestic products plus the value of its exports, must also equal the domestic sales of its domestic products plus the value of its imports. Hence the value of the country's exports must equal the value of its imports.

3. We have produced graphs that extend the analysis to three countries and that yield what are basically the same qualitative conclusions as those for the two-country case. These are provided in chapter 9.

4. There is a residual problem here. The wage rate so obtained depends on the employment figures, the employment figures depend on world demand, and world demand depends on the wage rate. However, it is easy to show that this yields a one-variable (linear) equation that can be used to solve for the wage rate.

5. If one is testing for local rather than global stability, the attempted entry that is tested for reversal by market forces must be on a small scale by hypothesis; otherwise, the deviation from the initial equilibrium will, by definition, not be small, so the change in question will not be local.

Chapter 7

This chapter provides some of the technical details of the analysis in chapter 3 of part I of this book.

1. If our graph is expressed in terms of a country's cardinal utility rather than its absolute income, exactly the same analysis clearly applies if the country's utility is a monotonically increasing function of its absolute income, and the qualitative properties of the frontiers are unchanged. Clearly, however, if utility is ordinal, conclusions about concavity of the frontiers cannot hold.

2. For a rigorous derivation of the shape of the frontier under assumptions that are somewhat more restrictive, see Gomory and Baumol (1996).

3. In carrying out our calculations, the mathematical program does not employ the full set of equilibrium conditions. Rather, it employs a single linear constraint that is consistent with these conditions. This constraint asserts simply that the share of world income accruing to a given country is equal to the sum of that country's share of world expenditures on the different goods it produces. This single constraint and its role is explained later in this chapter.

4. We also have a (more complicated) integer programming calculation that perfectly matches the boundary.

5. In an unpublished paper, Avinash Dixit has shown that convexity is sufficient but not necessary for scale economies.

Chapter 8

1. For easier reading, as the discussion here proceeds, from time to time the pertinent results of chapter 4 will be recapitulated.

2. The results of this chapter also apply to a world of diminishing returns, and not just to the linear case. To show this, it is only necessary to approximate such production functions by dividing them into linear segments. The linear programming technique described below for analysis of the purely linear case ensures that the segments will be used in the right order, with the most productive utilized first and the next most productive adopted only after its predecessor has been used to capacity. That is obviously in line with Ricardo's observation that the market will first make use of the most productive lands.

This piecewise linear approach does not work in the case of scale economies, since the mathematics would again try to use the most productive segments of the production function first. But that is impossible under scale economies, where productivity increases only after output has reached a large volume, that is, after having passed the small output levels with their low productivity.

Chapter 9

1. A similar argument applies to the zone of pure cooperation. It is also readily extended to the n country case where the relative volumes of these two zones are, for analogous reasons, multiplied by r^n, for some $r < 1$. This, in essence, is the logic that underlies proposition 2.

2. The analysis is provided in some detail in Gomory and Baumol (1992).

3. The analysis in the text can readily be extended to make it generally applicable to the case of a few large producers. There we can expect the marginal revenues of expanded production of a homogeneous commodity to be equal for all producers. Since profit maximization requires each producer's marginal cost to be equal to its marginal revenue, it follows here also that the marginal costs of all producers of a given good must be equal in equilibrium.

4. A second reservation is pertinent here. If the number of industries in the model is very small, an expansion of industry I in country 1 can raise country 1 wages, thereby offsetting the reduction in costs resulting from scale economies, and the opposite can be true in country 2 as a result of a decrease in its output of good I. Obviously, however, where

good *I* constitutes only a small share of a country's total output of all goods, a change in the production of good *I* will have only a negligible effect on that country's overall wage rate, so this second reservation will not be relevant.

5. Where the ratios between total purchase and minimum or maximum efficient scale are not integers, the analysis requires minor modifications. For details and extension of the analysis to determination of the efficient number of suppliers where each supplier provides a multiplicity of products, see Baumol, Panzar, and Willig (1988, chs. 2 and 5).

Chapter 10

1. For the classic survey of work in the area before the mid-1960s, see Chipman (1965). A very helpful summary of pertinent work of more recent vintage is provided in Bhagwati and Srinivasan (1983). For a fine survey-history of the debate between proponents of free trade and advocates of protection, see Douglas A. Irwin (1996).

2. Pigou adds: "Benefit might also be secured by a *permanent* bounty at a different rate from that contemplated above, so arranged as to force the industrial system from the summit of the hill-top on which it is found to any position, that overtops its present site, on the slope of a higher hill."

These observations, incidentally, draw attention to the more recent literature (going back to the work of Tibor Scitovsky) on "optimal tariffs," that is, the tariff levels that most effectively benefit the countries that adopt them.

3. Thus Graham showed that free trade equilibrium can leave a country worse off than it would be in autarky. We add the proof (chapter 7) that under scale economies there will always be such equilibria that are both undesirable and stable, and that when the number of traded goods is not small there will be many such equilibria.

4. Recent writers, particularly those using game-theoretic approaches, have emphasized that scale economies are not necessarily incompatible with the coexistence of a small number of rival firms. Each can adopt strategies that effectively prevent others from driving it out of the market. Even if this is a realistic possibility, it entails no conflict with our analysis. Our analysis does not require the absence of unspecialized equilibria. It only requires that in the presence of scale economies of the sort considered, every possible specialized assignment is a potential equilibrium.

5. Although Marshall apparently coined the term "external economies," he was hardly the first to discuss the concept (e.g., it occurs in Adam Smith's *An Inquiry into the Nature and Causes of the Wealth of Nations*, E. Cannan, ed., vol. 1, p. 307). More surprisingly, perhaps, Marshall does not seem to have discussed the concept or its implications to any considerable extent, either in the *Principles of Economics* or in his other books, rather, leaving the task to Pigou.

6. As Viner later realized after the matter was discussed with him by his draftsman, the mathematician Y. K. Wong, this argument is not quite right. The correct point is that when marginal cost is declining, the MC curve must cut the horizontal demand curve of the firm from above, thereby making it profitable for the firm to expand its output from the level at which MC equals price.

7. There are several reasons why scale economies need not always lead to perfect specialization and monopoly. In international trade, in the country that benefits from them,

wages may also be raised by expanding exports of the goods in question, thereby possibly offsetting the competitive benefits of the scale economies if they are relatively weak. Or rival producer countries of a good may each possess special advantages such as helpful natural resources that enable each to retain a position in the market. In the case of scale economies internal to firms, game theory tells us that a set of rival firms can adopt strategies that enable them all to survive, most obviously by entering into a cartel arrangement, though the stability of such an arrangement may be a delicate matter.

8. The intuitive argument is not quite right as it stands, but it is appropriately suggestive.

9. But Bhagwati's work on immiserizing growth (1958) should give us some reason for concern about this conclusion.

10. A fundamental assumption here, it will be recalled, is that all of the productivity parameters are bounded in each industry in each country by some natural or technological limit. Specifically, the analysis considers all average productivity values to satisfy $e_{i,j} \leq e_{i,j}^{max}$. A similar assumption is employed by Krugman (1985, p. 38), but is used by him for a different purpose.

11. See also the citations to the mercantilist literature and the illuminating quotations in Irwin (1996, pp. 116–118). Irwin also emphasizes the contributions to the literature by John Rae, William G. Sumner, Henry Sidgwick, C. F. Bastable, Paul-Gustave Fauveau, Frank Taussig, and James Meade (ch. 8). In our view, Irwin does not give adequate credit for originality and penetration to Alexander Hamilton. Also noteworthy is Irwin's conclusion that "a specific theoretical rationale for infant industry protection was never worked out" (p. 230).

12. Schumpeter (1954, p. 505) tells us: ". . . as regards his best-known contribution to the education of German public opinion on economic policy, the infant-industry argument, this is clearly Hamiltonian and part of the economic wisdom List imbibed during his stay in the United States."

13. This was not so in earlier models of trade in differentiated products because they assumed entry to be unrestricted and firms to be symmetrical.

14. Our results do not depend on the zero-profit assumption, though it does make the mathematics easier. One can modify our model by dropping the externalities premise and taking each commodity to be produced by a monopoly as a result of the scale economies. One can then substitute for the requirement of zero profit in each industry a set of profit-maximization conditions, essentially asserting that in each industry marginal cost equals marginal revenue.

15. Even here there are, in a general sense, predecessors. Thus, while Cournot, for example, uses calculus techniques in his comparative statics analysis of the effect of a change in cost on monopoly price (1838, 1929, pp. 61–62), Marshall employs a graphic comparative statics analysis, as we do (*Principles*, bk. V, ch. xiv). As a result he can deal effectively (if somewhat clumsily) with larger changes and global as well as local maxima, even when the usual concavity assumption for the profit function does not hold (e.g., see note 1 on pp. 483–484).

Chapter 11

1. We should presumably expect something similar to emerge from the static (neo)classical model of international trade with its assumption of constant or diminishing returns

to scale and its unique equilibrium. Since in this model, unlike that with scale economies or high entry costs, the apportionment of the task of production of each commodity is governed entirely by comparative advantage, a *ceteris paribus* trend toward equalization of factor proportions should reduce the forces, making for specialization of the individual trading countries in different sets of products, and should lead to increased similarity among countries in their product lines.

2. This index is analogous to Balassa's Revealed Comparative Advantage (RCA) measure (Balassa 1965), which is used to measure trade specialization.

3. RELPSHR is defined as a country's share of total output of a particular industry relative to a country's share of total GDP, rather than relative to its share of total manufacturing output. This is to avoid distortion as a result of the fact that some countries, such as Germany in 1970 and Japan in 1993, had specialized in production in manufacturing far more than other countries. Countries with a large manufacturing sector will, clearly, tend to have a large number of industries with values of RELPSHR exceeding unity.

4. R&D intensity is measured by the share of R&D outlays relative to sales of the sector.

5. One unfortunate property of the RELPSHR measure is that it is both asymmetric and highly skewed, with a range from zero to infinity. As a result industry production shares greater than average receive greater weight in the computation of the correlation coefficient than those less than average (which range in value from 0.0 to 1.0). A better measure is the logarithm of RELPSHR, which has a more normal distribution and gives equal weight to production shares both below and above average.

6. Since the cross-country average value of LN(RELPSHR) is generally zero (the average value of RELPSHR is one), the sum of squared values is similar to a variance measure, showing how different a country's industry production is from the average for the 14 countries.

Annotated Bibliography of Relevant Articles by Gomory and Baumol

1. A Ricardo model with economies of scale, *C.V. Starr Economic Research Report (New York University)* (Ralph E. Gomory). June 1992, RR # 92-29. This is the most complete and detailed discussion of the scale economies model. The equilibrium model is described in detail and both linear and integer programming approaches are given. Nonspecialized equilibria are discussed in detail.

2. Scale economies, the regions of multiple trade equilibria, and gains from acquisition of industries (Ralph E. Gomory and William J. Baumol), *C.V. Starr Economic Research Report* (New York University), June 1992, RR # 92-10. This report recapitulates the salient features of the scale economies model and introduces the analysis for the case where some industries have economies of scale and some have diseconomies.

3. Toward a theory of industrial policy-retainable industries (Ralph E. Gomory and William J. Baumol), *C.V. Starr Economic Research Report (New York University)*, December 1992, RR # 92-54. This introduces the concept of retainable industry and discusses the related policy implications.

4. A Ricardo model with economies of scale (Ralph E. Gomory), *Journal of Economic Theory*, April 1994, Vol. 62, No. 2, pp. 394–419. This is a publication length version of (1) above. It contains a careful discussion of equilibria and the main methods of calculating them, and their economic meaning.

5. A linear Ricardo model with varying parameters (Ralph E. Gomory and William J. Baumol), *Proceedings of the National Academy of Sciences*, USA, 1995, Vol. 92, pp. 1205–1207. This paper introduces the linear production model, and summarizes the principal results, notably similarity of both equations and results to those already obtained for industries with economies of scale.

6. Inefficient and locally stable trade equilibria under scale economies: Comparative advantage revisited (William J. Baumol and Ralph E. Gomory) published in *KYKLOS, International Review for Social Sciences*, Switzerland, 1996, Vol. 49, Fasc. 4, pp. 509–540. With so many different equilibria in economies of scale models it is natural to ask which of the many POSSIBLE equilibria are efficient. A very careful analysis of the efficiency and degree of efficiency of the various equilibria is given.

7. Productivity differences, world-market shares and conflicting national interests in linear trade models (Ralph E. Gomory and William J. Baumol), *Japan and the World Economy*, International Journal of Theory and Policy, Elsevier Science Publishers B.V. (North Holland), Vol. 9 (1997), pp. 123–150. This is a readable summary of many of the

principal aspects of the economies and linear models with emphasis on the latter. It includes a discussion of the correspondence principle.

8. Analysis of linear trade models and relation to scale economies (Ralph E. Gomory and William J. Baumol), *Proceedings of the National Academy of Sciences*, USA, 1997, Vol. 94, pp. 10002–10005. This paper introduces the integer programming description of the boundaries that gives the boundaries exactly for both large and small models. The correspondence principle is discussed.

9. National trade conflicts caused by productivity changes: The analysis with full proofs (Ralph E. Gomory and William J. Baumol), *C.V. Starr Economic Research Report* (New York University), November 1998, RR # 98-35. This is a very complete discussion of the linear model. It contains the equilibrium conditions, the exact boundary characterization through integer programming, a detailed discussion of the correspondence principle, and actual formulas for the boundaries with symmetric demand. It also introduces a simple diagram making an immediate connection between the structure of a country's industries and the shape of the boundary curve.

10. National trade conflicts caused by productivity changes (Ralph E. Gomory and William J. Baumol), *C.V. Starr Economic Research Report* (New York University), November 1998, RR # 98-36. This is a publication length and more readable version of the article above (9) to which it often refers for proofs and additional material.

References

Arthur, W. Brian. 1989. Competing technologies, increasing returns and lock in by historical events. *Economic Journal* 99: 116–31.

Arrow, Kenneth. 1962. The economic implications of learning by doing. *Review of Economic Studies* 29: 155–73.

Balassa, Bela. 1965. Trade liberalization and "revealed" comparative advantage. *The Manchester School* 33: 99–123.

Baumol, William J., John C. Panzar, and Robert D. Willig. 1988. *Contestable Markets and the Theory of Industry Structure*, rev. ed. San Diego: Harcourt Brace Jovanovich.

Bhagwati, Jagdish N. 1958. Immiserizing growth: A geometrical note. *Review of Economic Studies* 25: 201–5.

Bhagwati, Jagdish, and T. N. Srinivasan. 1983. *Lectures on International Trade*. Cambridge: MIT Press, ch. 26.

Chandler, Alfred. 1977. *The Visible Hand: The Managerial Revolution in American Business*. Cambridge: Belknap Press.

Chichilnisky, Graciela, and Geoffrey Heal. 1986. *The Evolving International Economy*. Cambridge: Cambridge University Press.

Chipman, John S. 1965. A survey of the theory of international trade: Part 2, The neoclassical theory. *Econometrica* 33: 685–760.

Corden, Warner M. 1956. Economic expansion and international trade: A geometric approach. *Oxford Economic Papers* 8: 223–28.

Cournot, A. A. 1838. *The Mathematical Principles of the Theory of Wealth*. English trans., New York: Macmillan Company, 1897.

David, Paul. 1985. Clio and the economics of Qwerty. *American Economic Review* 35: 332–37.

Dixit, Avinash K., and Victor D. Norman. 1980. *Theory of International Trade*. Cambridge: Cambridge University Press.

Dollar, David, and Edward N. Wolff. 1993. *Competitiveness, Convergence, and International Specialization*. Cambridge: MIT Press.

Dornbush, Rudiger W., Stanley Fischer, and Paul A. Samuelson. 1977. Comparative advantage, trade and payments in a Ricardian model with a continuum of goods. *American Economic Review* 67: 823–39.

Edgeworth, F. Y. 1925. *Papers Relating to Political Economy*. London: Macmillan.

Ethier, Wilfred J. 1979. Internationally decreasing costs and world trade. *Journal of International Economics* 9: 1–24.

Ethier, Wilfred J. 1982. Decreasing costs in international trade and Frank Graham's argument for protection. *Econometrica* 50: 1243–68.

Findlay, Ronald, and Harry Grubert. 1959. Factor intensities, technological progress and the terms of trade. *Oxford Economic Papers* 11: 111–21.

Graham, Frank. 1923. Some aspects of protection further considered. *Quarterly Journal of Economics* 37: 199–227.

Grossman, Gene M., and Elhanan Helpman. 1991. *Innovation and Growth in the Global Economy*. Cambridge: MIT Press.

Hamilton, Alexander. 1791. *Report on Manufactures*. Communicated to the U.S. House of Representatives, December 5, 1791. Reprinted in S. McKee, ed. *Papers on Public Credit and Finance by Alexander Hamilton*. New York: Columbia University Press, 1934.

Helpman, Elhanan. 1984. Increasing returns, imperfect markets, and trade theory. In Ronald W. Jones and Peter B. Kenen, eds., *Handbook of International Economics*, vol. 1. Amsterdam: North Holland, pp. 325–65.

Helpman, Elhanan. 1994. Technology and trade. Working Paper 4926. National Bureau of Economic Research, Cambridge, MA.

Helpman, Elhanan, and Paul R. Krugman. 1985. *Market Structure and Foreign Trade*. Cambridge: MIT Press, 1985.

Hicks, J. R. 1953. An inaugural lecture. *Oxford Economic Papers* 5: 117–35.

Hicks, J. R., and R. G. D. Allen. 1934. A reconsideration of the theory of value. *Economica* 1: 52–76, 196–219.

Hume, David. 1741–42. *Essays, Literary, Moral and Political*. Edinburgh: Alexander Kincaid. Volume 1, 1741, volume 2, 1742; reprinted with corrections and additions, 1748.

Hymans, S. H., and F. P. Stafford. 1995. Divergence, convergence, and the gains from trade. *Review of International Economics* 3: 118–23.

Irwin, Douglas A. 1996. *Against the Tide: An Intellectual History of Free Trade*. Princeton: Princeton University Press.

Johnson, G. E., and F. P. Stafford. 1993. International competition and real wages. *American Economic Review* 83: 127–30.

Johnson, G. E., and F. P. Stafford. 1998. Technology regimes and the distribution of real wages. In Gunnar Eliasson and Christopher Green, eds., *Microfoundations of Economic Growth: A Schumpeterian Perspective*. Ann Arbor, MI: University of Michigan Press, pp. 348–68.

Johnson, Harry G. 1955. Economic expansion and international trade. *Manchester School of Economic and Social Studies* 95–112.

Johnson, Harry G. 1971. *Aspects of the Theory of Tariffs*. Cambridge: Harvard University Press.

Kahn, Alfred E. 1988. *The Economics of Regulation*. Cambridge: MIT Press 2nd ed.

Kaserman, D. L., and J. H. Mayo. 1995. *Government and Business: The Economics of Antitrust and Regulation*. Fort Worth, TX: Dryden Press.

Kemp, M. C. 1964. *The Pure Theory of International Trade*. Englewood Cliffs, NJ: Prentice Hall.

Knight, Frank H. 1924. Some fallacies in the interpretation of social cost. *Quarterly Journal of Economics* 38: 582–606.

Krugman, Paul R. 1979. Increasing returns, monopolistic competition and international trade. *Journal of International Economics* 9: 469–79.

Krugman, Paul R. 1983. Targeted industrial policies: Theory and evidence. *Industrial Change and Public Policy*. Kansas City, MO: Federal Reserve Bank, pp. 123–55.

Krugman, Paul R. 1984. The U.S. response to foreign industrial targeting and the U.S. economy. *Brookings Papers on Economic Activity*, Spring: 77–121.

Krugman, Paul R. 1985. A "Technology Gap" Model of International Trade. In K. Jungenfelt and D. Hague, eds., *Structural Adjustment in Developed Open Economies*. New York: St. Martin's Press, pp. 35–49.

Krugman, Paul R. 1987. Is free trade passé? *Journal of Economic Perspectives* 1: 131–44.

Krugman, Paul R. 1991. History versus expectations. *Quarterly Journal of Economics* 106: 651–67.

Krugman, Paul R., and Robert Lawrence. 1993. Trade, jobs and wages. Working Paper 4478. National Bureau of Economic Research. Cambridge, MA.

Krugman, Paul R., and A. Venables. 1992. Integration, specialization and adjustment. Centre for Economic Performance, London School of Economics.

Landes, David. 1969. *The Unbound Prometheus*. Cambridge: Cambridge University Press.

List, Friedrich. 1841. *Die Theorie das Nationalen Systems der Politischen Öeconomie*, Stuttgart Verlag der königl. hofbuchhandlung von Julius Weise, English trans., 1885.

Marshall, Alfred. 1879. *Pure Theory (Foreign Trade—Domestic Values)*. Privately printed 1879, Reprinted, London School of Economics, 1930.

Marshall, Alfred. 1890–1920. *Principles of Economics*. London: Macmillan. First edition published 1890, 8th edition 1920.

Matthews, R. C. O. 1949–50. Reciprocal demand and increasing returns. *Review of Economic Studies* 17: 149–58.

McCloskey, D. N. 1981. *Enterprise and Trade in Victorian Britain*. London: George Allen and Unwin.

Meade, J. E. 1952. *A Geometry of International Trade*. London: George Allen and Unwin.

Mill, John Stuart. *Principles of Political Economy*, rev. ed. New York: Colonial Press. First edition published 1848.

Mishan, E. J. 1955. The long-run dollar problem: A comment. *Oxford Economic Papers* 7: 215–20.

Nadiri, M. Ishaq, and Banani Nandi. 1999. Benefits of communications infrastructure capital in U.S. economy. (Forthcoming in *Economics of Innovation and New Technology*), December.

Pigou, A. C. 1906. *Protective and Preferential Import Duties*. London: Macmillan.

Pigou, A. C. 1932. *The Economics of Welfare*, 4th ed. London: Macmillan.

Romer, Paul. 1994. New goods, old theory and the welfare costs of trade restrictions. *Journal of Development Economics* 43: 5–38.

Roy, R. 1942. *De l'Utilité: Contribution a la théorie des choix*. Paris.

Samuelson, Paul A. 1953. Consumption theorems in terms of overcompensation rather than indifference comparisons. *Economica* 20: 1–9.

Scitovsky, Tibor. 1947. A reconsideration of the theory of tariffs. *Review of Economic Studies* 9: 89–110.

Sharkey, W. 1982. *The Theory of Natural Monopoly*. Cambridge: Cambridge University Press.

Spencer, Barbara J., and James A. Brander. 1983. International R&D rivalry and industrial strategy. *Review of Economic Studies* 50: 707–22.

Smith, Adam. 1776. *An Inquiry into the Nature and Causes of the Wealth of Nations*, Edwin Cannan, ed., London: Methuen, 1904.

Summers, Robert, and Alan Heston. 1991. The Penn World Table (Mark 5): An expanded set of international comparisons, 1950–1988. *Quarterly Journal of Economics* 106: 327–68. Also available at: http://pwt.econ.upenn.edu.

Tyson, Laura d'Andrea. 1992. *Who's Bashing Whom: Trade Conflict on High Technology Industries*. Washington, DC: Institute for International Economics.

Viner, Jacob. 1931. Cost curves and supply curves. *Zeitschrift für Nationalöconomie* 3: 23–46.

Viner, Jacob. 1937. *Studies in the Theory of International Trade*. New York: Harper.

Viner, Jacob. 1950. *The Customs Union Issue*. New York: Carnegie Endowment for the International Peace.

Wicksell, Knut. 1901. *Lectures on Political Economy*. London: Routledge. English translation of the third edition, 1934.

Index

Acquired skills, 9–10, 42, 43, 48, 56, 63
Advantages
 acquired, xi, 7
 of established industry, 17 (*see also* Retainable industries)
African nations, in zone of mutual gains with U.S., 61
Airbus consortium, 63
Analytic tools, predecessors on, 158–60
Appropriate assignments, 30
Arthur, Brian, 148
Asian countries. *See also* China; Japan
 industrial success of, 42
 uneven productivity of, 53–54
 in zone of mutual gains with U.S., 61
Asymmetry, between advanced and less-developed countries, 126, 152–53
Athletic-shoe production, acquisition of, 64
Australia, and specialization, 166, 167, 173
Autarky, 96, 101
Auto industry
 Japanese, 17, 20, 176
 U.S. government intervention for, 67, 68
Average cost curve, flat-bottomed, 131–35

Balance-of-trade requirement, 181n.2
Baumol, William, annotated bibliography, 187–88
Belgium
 GDP of vs. U.S., 61
 and specialization, 166, 167, 171, 173
Biotech industry, 55, 66
Brander, James A., 157
Brazil, government support in, 63

Canada, and specialization, 167, 172, 173
Chandler, Alfred, 15
Changing industrial capabilities, 42
 and multiple outcomes, 43–44
Chemical industry, 176
Chichilnisky, Graciela, 160
China
 diminishing returns to scale for agriculture in, 14
 vs. Japan, 20
 in zone of mutual gains with U.S., 61
Chipman, John, 147
Classical trade models, 4, 5–6, 9, 10–11, 13, 177–78n.1
 absence of economies of scale in, 43, 81, 99–100
 diminishing returns to scale in, 14–15
Closing of markets to foreign competition, 8. *See also* Protection
Colbert, Jean-Baptiste, 156
Comparative advantage, 84, 163
Comparative statics analysis, 159, 159–160
Competition, with flat-bottomed average-cost curve, 134, 141
Conflicts in international trade, 24, 56, 57, 73, 141
 and equilibrium points, 36, 44, 53
 and level of development, 41–42, 100–101
 zone of, 37, 39, 60, 120–22, 140
Constant returns to scale. *See also* Linear production model
 in classical model, 99–100
 in flat-bottomed average cost curve, 131–35
 and pattern of outcomes, 97

Convergence, of production patterns, 164, 165–67
Correspondence theorems or principle, 107–109, 154
Cost curve, flat-bottomed average, 131–35
"Cost Curves and Supply Curves" (Viner), 150
Cournot, A. A., 149, 159
Cross-country dispersion, 167–73

Denmark
 GDP of vs. U.S., 61
 and specialization, 166, 167, 172
Developed countries
 as benefiting from aid to underdeveloped countries, 4, 41, 56, 69, 73, 100–101
 as benefiting from competition with other developed countries, 4, 41–42, 56
 as trading with unevenly developed countries, 53–55
Developing countries. See Underdeveloped countries
Diminishing returns to scale, 14–16, 118, 125–30, 140, 182n.2
Dispersion, cross-country, 167–73
Divided industries, 135–38
Dornbush, Rudiger W., 99, 152, 154, 159

Economics of Welfare (Pigou), 144, 147
Economies of scale, 13, 130–31, 154
 as assumption, 117–18
 bounded, 131–33
 and conflict, 24
 and correspondence theorems, 107–109, 154
 and country's acquisition of industries, 129, 130
 erosion of, 93
 vs. fragmentation of labor, 30
 in Marshall's analysis, 145–46
 in model of international trade, 77, 84, 85
 and multiple outcomes, 13–14
 and natural monopoly, 148–50
 predecessors on, 157–58
 as retainability, 42 (see also Retainable industries)
 and specialization, 151, 163, 184n.7
 and specialized equilibria, 78
Economists, vs. intuition of nonexperts, 3

Edgeworth, F. Y., 149–50, 161
Efficient scale, maximum and minimum, 133–34
Entertainmemt industry, internationalization of, 140
Entrepreneurship, in U.S. culture, 66
Entry
 with flat-bottomed average-cost curve, 134–35
 and markets closed to foreign competition, 8
 modern technology makes difficult, 6
 for retainable industries, 16–17, 19, 70 (see also Retainable industries)
Equal marginal-cost ratios, 126–27, 130
Equilibrium(a), 15, 77. See also Multiple outcomes of free international trade
 ideal, 40
 maximal-productivity, 102–103
 nonspecialized or imperfectly specialized, 87, 91–93
 perfectly specialized, 18, 78, 87, 91–93, 100, 117, 130, 148–51
Ethier, Wilfred, 156, 158
European Airbus consortium, 63

Filling-in theorem, 90–91
Finland, and specialization, 166, 167, 171
Fischer, Stanley, 99, 152, 154, 159
Flat-bottomed average cost curve, 131–35
Foreign industries. See also Trading partner
 closing of market to, 8 (see also Protection)
 and national well-being, 24–26, 41 (see also Gains from trade; Losses from trade; Trading partner)
France
 GDP of vs. U.S., 61
 government support in, 63
 and specialization, 167
Free trade (free market), 72–73
 acceptance of, 160–61
 classical model of, 4, 5–6, 10–11, 13, 177–78n.1 (see also Classical trade models)
 equilibrium in, 15
 Hamilton on, 155–56
 recent reservations about, 157
 variety of outcomes in, vi, 5, 7–8 (see also Multiple outcomes of free international trade)

Gains from trade, 30. *See also* Zones of
   mutual gains
GDP (gross domestic product), and
   country's position in distribution of
   trade outcomes, 61
Germany
 GDP of vs. U.S., 61
 and specialization, 165–66, 167, 168–70,
   173
Global acquisition of skills, 9–10, 43, 48,
   56, 63
Global trade. *See* International trade
Gomory, Ralph, annotated bibliography,
   187–88
Government role in economic
   development, 57, 58, 63, 65
 in developing nations, 71
 infrastructure development, 69
 predecessors on, 147, 154–57, 160–61
 for productivity improvement, 69
 in U.S., 65–67
Graham, Frank, 147, 150, 156
Greece, and U.S. ideal trading partner,
   62
Grossman, Gene M., 157, 159

Hamilton, Alexander, 143, 155–56
Heal, Geoffrey, 160
Heckscher-Ohlin model, 164, 175
Helpman, Elhanan, 157, 159
Hicks, J. R., 99, 151–52, 159–60
High startup costs. *See* Startup costs
High technology industries, 55
 emphasis on as desirable, 64
Historical accidents
 and outcomes, 20, 148
 industrial dominance through, 7
 and specialization, 176
Hume, David, quoted, 143

Ideal equilibria, 40
Ideal trading partner, 54, 100, 109–13, 153
Imperfectly specialized equilibria, 91–93
Income per person, and country's
   position in distribution of trade
   outcomes, 61
Increasing internal returns to scale (IIRS),
   163. *See also* Economies of scale
Industrial design, internationalization of,
   140
Industrial dominance, through historical
   accident, 7

Industrial policy
 of Japan, 176
 and U.S., 65, 66
Industrial Revolution, cost of machinery
   in, 14–15
Infant industry argument, 25, 154–56
Infrastructure development, 69
Integer programming, in model of
   international trade, 89
Integer programming problem, xii
Internationalization
 of companies, 177n.3
 of industries, 140
International trade
 changes in, xi
 classical models of, 4, 5–6, 9, 10–11, 13,
   177–78n.1 (*see also* Classical trade
   models)
 conflicts in, 24, 57, 73, 141 (*see also*
   Conflicts in international trade)
 and diminishing returns, 15–16 (*see also*
   Diminishing returns to scale)
 and distinctive attributes of modern
   industry, 57
 and economies of scale, 13–14, 130–31,
   154 (*see also* Economies of scale)
 and increased abilities of trading
   partner, 41
 model of, 77–81 (*see also* Model of
   international trade)
 multiple outcomes of, vi, 7–9, 21–22,
   23–40, 73, 83 (*see also* Multiple
   outcomes of free international trade)
 need to modify theory of, xi
 overall benefit vs. localized pain of, 3
 retainable industries in, 16–17, 164, 176
   (*see also* Retainable industries)
 and welfare of country, 5
Internet, and government, 66, 67
Internet companies, 55
Invention, U.S. achievements in, 66
Investment, and U.S. venture capital
   system, 66
Investment in research and development,
   175–76
Invisible Hand, 11, 13, 15, 16
 and imperfect welfare, 94
 and local stability, 17
Irwin, Douglas, 160
Italy
 GDP of vs. U.S., 61
 and specialization, 166, 173

Japan
  auto industry in, 17, 20, 176
  government support in, 63
  industrial policy of, 176
  and specialization, 166, 166–67, 168–70,
    171, 172, 173
  steelmaking in, 20
Johnson, Harry, 161

Kemp, M. C., 158
Keynes, John Maynard, 161
Knight, Frank, 150
Korea. See South Korea
Krugman, Paul, 99, 148, 150–51, 152–53,
  157, 159, 160

Landes, David, 14
Latin American nations, in zone of
  mutual gains with U.S., 61
Learning-by-doing, 17, 163
Less developed countries. See
  Underdeveloped countries
Linear production, 43–44
  in mixture, 124–25
Linear production model, 44, 99–101
  correspondence theorems for, 107–109,
    154
  and evolution in country's productivity,
    113–16
  graphing of, 44–48, 101–104
  graphs of competing individual
    countries, 50–53
  and ideal trading partner, 109–13
  and more vs. less developed trading
    partners, 53–55, 56
  multiple equilibria in, 101
  and rapidly evolving industries, 55–56
  and region of maximal productivity,
    48–50
  two-industry vs. many-industry, 104–
    107
List, Friedrich, 154, 156
Literature on economics, pertinent
  strands in, 143–44. See also
  Predecessors
Living standards, raising of as essential
  task, 72
Location of economic activity, and
  economic benefit, xi-xii
Losses from trade, 3, 4, 24–26, 33, 101,
  182n.3

Many-industry models, vs. two-industry
  models, 104–107
Marginal costs, equality of, 127, 130
Market forces. See also Free trade;
  Multiple outcomes of free
  international trade
  in retainable industries, 17
  variety of outcomes from, 7–8
  in world of scale economies, 94
Marshall, Alfred, 144–47, 149, 158
Marshall Plan, 38–39
Maximal-productivity equilibria, 102–103
Maximum efficient scale, 133–34
Maximum productivity outcomes, 48–50
Mercantilists, 161
Metallurgy, 67
Mexico
  and ideal U.S. trading partner, 62
  low wages in, 42
Mill, John Stuart, 149, 154, 156
Minimum efficient scale, 133–34
Model of international trade, 77–81. See
  also Classical trade models; Linear
  production model; Multiple outcomes
  of free international trade
  and advantages of initial leadership, 175
  assumptions in, 77–78, 117–18
  with diminishing returns to scale,
    125–30
  divided (shared) industries in, 135–38
  with mixture of retainable and linear-
    production industries, 124–25
  and nontraded goods, 125, 138–40
  one vs. many producers in, 130
  questions on, 57–59
  and scale economies, 130–31
    bounded, 131, 140–41
    and flat-bottomed average cost curve,
      131–35
  variables of, 88
Models, economic
  and free trade, 5
  simplifying function of, 3
Monopoly privileges, for trading
  companies, 154–55
Multi-country cases. See Three-country
  models
Multinational corporations, 9–10
  acquisition of skills from, 63
  and home countries, 71–72
  and trading-partner development, 69

Multiple outcomes (equilibria) of free
    international trade, vi, 7–9
and acquired advantage, 7
and action to modify outcome, 11
and economies of scale, 13–14
and entry problem, 6, 7, 8, 9
for linear models, 101
pattern of, 21–22, 23–40, 73, 83 (*see also*
    Pattern of multiple outcomes from
    trade)
predecessors on, 144–48, 156
and productivity growth, 9–10, 43–56
  in country's trading partners, 41, 53–55,
    56, 99, 101, 111–12, 113–116
range of opposed and of complementary
    interests, 52–53
and retainable industries, 18–19 (*see also*
    Retainable industries)
as vast number of equilibria, 7, 19, 81,
    178n.4
and welfare of country, 19–21, 40
and welfare of world, 20–21, 40
Multiple possibilities, zones of, 120–122
Mutual gains, zones of, 37, 39, 59–60,
    120–22, 140, 141

"Natural monopoly," 78, 148–50
Netherlands
 GDP of vs. U.S., 61
 and specialization, 166, 167, 173
Nonretainable industries, 68–69
 as targets for acquisition, 63–64
Nonspecialized equilibria, 87, 91–93
Nontraded goods, 125, 138–40
Norway
 GDP of vs. U.S., 61
 and specialization, 166, 167, 172
Number of traded goods, 81, 104–107,
    117, 159

Optimal tariffs, 183n.2
Outcomes of free trade. *See* Equilibrium;
    Multiple outcomes of free
    international trade; Pattern of
    multiple outcomes from trade

Patents of monopoly, 155
Pattern of multiple outcomes from trade,
    21–22, 23, 73, 83
 boundary determination for, 86–88,
    97–98

complications in, 88–89
simplifications of, 89–90
and tightness of boundaries, 90–91
conflict between nations, 24
country's knowledge of position in, 58,
    59–62
derivation of upper frontiers for, 83–86
disadvantage to country, 24–26, 33–35
graphical representation of, 26–39
and ideal equilibria (national vs. world),
    40
inefficiency in, 94–95
moving to better position in, 62–68
infrastucture development, 69
and less developed nations, 69–71
and nonretainable industries, 68–69
and welfare properties, 94, 95–97
zone of conflict, 37, 39, 60, 120–22,
    140
zones of mutual gains, 37, 39, 59–60,
    120–22, 140, 141
Per capita incomes, and country's
    position in distribution of trade
    outcomes, 61
Perfectly specialized equilibria, 18, 78, 87,
    91, 130
 as assumption, 117
 and linear model, 100
 predecessors on, 148–51
Perfectly specialized outcomes, as stable
    equilibria, 78–81
Pigou, A. C., 144, 147, 156, 160
Policy. *See* Government role in economic
    development; U.S. policy
Political Economy Club, 161
"Political problem," 65
Powdered metallurgy industry, 67
Predecessors, 143–44, 160
 Arthur, 148
 Chichilnisky and Heal, 160
 Chipman, 147
 Colbert, 156
 Cournot, 149, 159
 Dornbush, Fischer and Samuelson, 99,
    152, 154, 159
 Edgeworth, 149–50, 161
 Ethier, 156, 158
 Graham, 147, 150, 156
 Grossman, 157, 159
 Hamilton, 143, 155–56
 Helpman, 157, 159

Predecessors (cont.)
  Hicks, 99, 151–52, 159–60
  Hume (quoted), 143
  Johnson, 161
  Kemp, 158
  Keynes, 161
  Knight, 150
  Krugman, 99, 148, 150–51, 152–53, 157,
    159, 160
  List, 154, 156
  Marshall, 144–47, 149, 158
  Mill, 149, 154, 156
  Pigou, 144, 147, 156, 160
  Roberts, 161
  Romer, 147–48
  Sharkey, 150
  Sidgwick, 161
  Smith, 11, 15, 161
  Spencer and Brander, 157
  Stafford et al., 99, 113, 153
  Torrens, 161
  Venables, 150–51
  Viner, 150, 154–55
  Wicksell, 150
Production patterns, convergence of, 164,
  165–67
Productivity
  limits on, 45–46, 55
  relative, 179n.8
Productivity effect, 106
Productivity growth
  and changing capabilities, 42–44
  effect of on trading partner, 41–42, 55,
    56, 99, 101, 111–12, 113–16
  and predecessors, 151–53
  in linear models, 43–56, 113–16, 154 (see
    also Linear production model)
  and multiple economic outcomes, 9–10,
    43–56
  predecessors on, 151–54
  in rapidly evolving industries, 55
  in selected industries (Far East), 69–70
  and world output, 47–48, 151
Protection
  Graham on, 147
  infant industry argument for, 25, 154–56
  as issue, 161
  and Japanese auto industry, 17
  Pigou on, 144

Rapidly evolving industries, 55–56, 56
Region of maximal productivity, 48–50

Relative advantage or productivity, 55,
  179n.8
RELPSHR (relative production measure),
  165, 170n.a, 185nn.3, 5, 6
Research
  investment in, 175–76
  for U.S. industries, 66–67
Retainable industries (retainability), 17,
  42, 164, 176
  as advantage against developing
    countries, 53
  alternative equilibria from, 18–19
  as double-edged sword, 70
  focus on as desirable, 64
  and infant-industry argument, 25
  in mixture, 124–25
  and prosperity of country, 21, 43
  as targets for acquisition, 63–64
Ricardo, David, xi, 3–4, 15, 84, 160
Roberts, Lewis, 161
Romer, Paul, 147–48

Samuelson, Paul A., 99, 152, 154, 159,
  159–60
Scale diseconomies. See Diminishing
  returns to scale
Scale economies. See Economies of scale
Scarf, Herbert, xii
Self-interest, as injuring trading partner,
  40, 57
Sematech, 67
Semiconductors, U.S. government
  intervention for, 67, 68
Shape of region of outcomes from trade.
  See Pattern of multiple outcomes from
  trade
Shared industries, 93, 135–38
Sharkey, William, 150
Sidgwick, Henry, 161
Singapore, selected industries developed
  in, 70
Skills, acquired, 9–10, 42, 43, 48, 56, 63
Smith, Adam, 11, 15, 161
South Korea
  government support in, 63
  and ideal trading partner for U.S., 62
  selected industries developed in, 70
Soviet economies, near-zero productivity
  of, 45
Specialization, 18–19, 163–64, 173–76
  and cross-country dispersion, 171
  indicator of, 165